MASTERING THE GRADE 3 ISAT READING AND WRITING TESTS

JAMES KILLORAN

STUART ZIMMER

MARK JARRETT

JARRETT PUBLISHING COMPANY

EAST COAST OFFICE
P.O. Box 1460
19 Cross Street
Ronkonkoma, NY 11779
631-981-4248

WEST COAST OFFICE
10 Folin Lane
Lafayette, CA 94549
925-906-9742

1-800-859-7679   Fax: 631-588-4722
www.jarrettpub.com

> This book includes material from many different sources. Occasionally it is not possible to determine if a particular source is copyrighted, and if so, who is the copyright owner. Every effort has been made to trace the ownership of all copyrighted material and to secure the necessary permissions to reprint these selections. If there has been a copyright infringement with any material in this book, it is unintentional. We extend our sincerest apologies and would be happy to make immediate and appropriate restitution upon proof of copyright ownership.

Grateful acknowledgment is made to the following to reprint the copyrighted materials listed below:

"Old Joe and the Carpenter" excerpted from *Thirty-Three Multi-cultural Tales To Tell,* © 1993 by Pleasant L. DeSpain. Used by permission of August House Publishers. Children's Better Health Institute for the article in *Child Life,* "Happy Birthday, Basketball" by Charles Davis in the March, 2000 issue. Cobblestone Publishing Company for the articles in *Appleseeds Magazine,* "Pass the Bread, Please" by Cyndy Hall and "School Days" by Joyce Haynes, both appearing in the February, 1999 issue. Harcourt, Brace, and Company for *Half Magic,* by Edward Eager, © 1954. *Highlights For Children* for: the story "The Recital" by Kathleen Benner Duble, in the February, 1999 issue; the story "Carrie Rose Hated Red" by Susan Uhlig, in the April, 2000 issue; the story, "Come Rain or Shine" a folktale retold by Geary Smith, in the March, 1995 issue; the article, "Chopsticks" by Samantha Bonar, in the September, 1995 issue; the article "Calm Under Fire: The Story of Henry Flipper" by Bea Bragg in the February, 1999 issue; the article "Treasure Hunter" by Ellen Hobart in the May, 2000 issue; the article "The Wandering Continent" by Eon Bilokur, in the June, 1955 issue; the article, "The Cold Facts About Ice Cream" by Kristin Martelle, in the August, 1995 issue. Scholastic, Inc. for the article in *Scholastic Update,* "The Deformed Frogs" by Susan Hayes, in the April 13, 1998 issue. Simon and Schuster for the story "Tashira's Turn" in *The Children's Book of Heroes* edited by William Bennett, © 1997. *Science Around the Year* by Janice Cleave © 2000. Reprinted by permission of Wiley-Liss, Inc., Jossey-Bass Inc., a subsidiary of John Wiley & Sons, Inc.

Copyright 2001 by Jarrett Publishing Company

All rights reserved. No part of this book may be reproduced in any form or by any means, including electronic, photographic, mechanical, or by any device for storage and retrieval of information, without the express written permission of the publisher. Requests for permission to copy any part of this book should be mailed to:

Jarrett Publishing Company
Post Office Box 1460
19 Cross Street
Ronkonkoma, New York 11779

ISBN 1-882422-62-7
Printed in the United States of America
by Malloy Lithographing, Inc., Ann Arbor, Michigan
First Edition
10 9 8 7 6 5 4 3 2 1   04 03 02 01

ACKNOWLEDGMENTS

The authors would like to thank the following educators who helped review the manuscript. Their collective comments, suggestions, and recommendations have proved invaluable in preparing this book.

Rosa Sailes
Department of Instruction, Medill Training Center
Administrator, Chicago Public Schools

Ruth Townsend
Teacher at Manhattanville College,
Purchase, New York
English Language Arts Consultant, N.Y.S.E.C. Teacher of Excellence
Director for the National Council of Teachers of English (Region 1)

Cover design, layout, graphics, and typesetting:
Burmar Technical Corporation, Albertson, N.Y.

This book is dedicated…

to my wife Donna, and my children Christian, Carrie, and Jesse
— *James Killoran*

to my wife Joan, my children Todd and Ronald, and
my grandchildren Jared and Katie
— *Stuart Zimmer*

to my wife Gośka, and my children Alexander and Julia
— *Mark Jarrett*

Other books by Killoran, Zimmer, and Jarrett
Mastering the Grade 5 ISAT Reading and Writing Test
Mastering the Grade 4 MCAS Tests in English Language Arts
Mastering the Grade 3 MCAS Reading Test
Mastering New York's Grade 4 English Language Arts Test
Mastering New York's Grade 8 English Language Arts Test
Mastering Ohio's Fourth Grade Proficiency Tests in Reading and Writing
Mastering the Grade 4 FCAT Reading and Writing Test
Mastering the Elementary English Language Arts
Introducing the Elementary English Language Arts

TABLE OF CONTENTS

UNIT 1: TOOLS FOR READING

CHAPTER 1: HOW TO BE A GOOD READER 2
Reading Strategies 2
Before Reading 3
During Reading 4
After Reading 5
A Sample Model 6

CHAPTER 2: TOOLS FOR UNDERSTANDING UNFAMILIAR WORDS AND PHRASES 8
Use Word Patterns to Sound Out the Word 8
Use Context Clues 12
Use Your Knowledge of Parts of Speech 15
Use Word Analysis 16
Applying What You Have Learned 18

CHAPTER 3: ADDITIONAL TOOLS FOR READING WITH UNDERSTANDING 19
Using Question Words 19
Using Graphic Organizers 23

UNIT 2: TYPES OF READINGS

CHAPTER 4: READING LITERARY TEXTS 29
The Parts of a Story 29

CHAPTER 5: READING INFORMATIONAL TEXTS 42
Types of Informational Readings 42
The Parts of an Informational Reading 45
The Main Idea of a Reading 47
Finding the Main Idea 47
The Supporting Details 49
Changing What You Have Read into a Graphic Organizer 49

UNIT 3: QUESTIONS ON THE READING TEST

INTRODUCTION TO ANSWERING MULTIPLE-CHOICE QUESTIONS ... 56

CHAPTER 6: QUESTIONS ON OPENING IMPRESSIONS 58
Literary Texts 58
Informational Texts 59

CHAPTER 7: QUESTIONS ON VOCABULARY AND
WORD ANALYSIS 63
Vocabulary Questions 63
Word Analysis Questions 66

CHAPTER 8: QUESTIONS ABOUT DETAILS IN A READING 72
Scanning to Find Answers 73
Fact and Opinion Questions 78

CHAPTER 9: QUESTIONS ABOUT CONNECTING DETAILS 82
Sequence Questions 83
Explanation Questions 85
Compare-and-Contrast Questions 88
Pulling-It-Together Questions 91
Prediction Questions 93

CHAPTER 10: QUESTIONS ON THE MAIN IDEA OR THEME 99
Finding the Main Idea of an Informational Reading 100
Finding the Theme of a Story 103

CHAPTER 11: ANSWERING EXTENDED-RESPONSE
QUESTIONS 107
Steps in Answering the Question 107
Types of Extended-Response Questions 108

CHAPTER 12: TESTING YOUR UNDERSTANDING 114
Session 1 114
Session 2 121

v

Unit 4: Writing

Introduction to Writing 130

CHAPTER 13: THE ELEMENTS OF GOOD WRITING 131
The Writing Prompt 132
Focus 133
Elaboration/Support 133
Organization 134
Writing Conventions 137

CHAPTER 14: RESPONDING TO A WRITING PROMPT 138
Steps in Responding to a Writing Prompt 138

CHAPTER 15: WRITING A NARRATIVE ESSAY 143
What is a Narrative Essay? 143
Hints for Writing a Narrative Essay 144
A Model Narrative Essay 149
Practice Writing a Narrative Essay 150

CHAPTER 16: WRITING AN EXPOSITORY ESSAY 155
What is an Expository Essay? 155
Hints for Writing an Expository Essay 156
A Model Expository Essay 160
Practice Writing a Expository Essay 162

CHAPTER 17: WRITING A PERSUASIVE ESSAY 166
What is a Persuasive Essay? 166
Hints for Writing a Persuasive Essay 167
A Model Persuasive Essay 170
Practice Writing a Persuasive Essay 172

Unit 5: Practice Tests

CHAPTER 18: A PRACTICE READING TEST 176

CHAPTER 19: A PRACTICE WRITING TEST 200

Appendix 203

UNIT 1: TOOLS FOR READING

📖 **Chapter 1:** How To Be a Good Reader

📖 **Chapter 2:** Tools for Understanding Unfamiliar Words and Phrases

📖 **Chapter 3:** Additional Tools for Reading with Understanding

---

The **Grade 3 ISAT Reading Test** will test your ability to read and understand different kinds of texts. The test includes both multiple-choice and short-answer questions. Specifically, the reading test will examine the following:

★ Your ability to use word analysis and vocabulary skills

★ Your ability to understand different types of readings

★ Your use of different reading strategies

★ Your understanding of literary elements and techniques

★ Your ability to read different types of literature

CHAPTER 1

HOW TO BE A GOOD READER

Are you a good reader? You probably first began to read by sounding out or memorizing words. However, recognizing words is just the beginning of being a good reader. The most important part of reading is **understanding** the ideas of the writer and seeing how these apply to your own ideas.

You should try to become an **active** reader. You can interact with what you read by asking questions. Think about how the author's ideas match your own ideas. This interacting with what you read helps you to understand the reading better. In this chapter, you will learn some important ways of thinking about what you read.

READING STRATEGIES

A **strategy** is a plan for achieving a goal. Just as a coach uses a strategy to win a game, good readers use special strategies when they read. Experts in reading have identified several strategies used by good readers to better understand and apply what they read. Using these strategies will help you improve your reading. It will also help you get a better score on the **Grade 3 ISAT Reading Test.**

STRATEGIES USED BY GOOD READERS

Make Connections
Good readers make connections with what they already know as they read.

Ask Questions
Good readers ask themselves questions about what they are reading.

Think about What's Important
Good readers think about what is important as they read.

Summarize
Good readers summarize the text in their own words as they read.

Make Predictions
Good readers make predictions and draw conclusions as they read.

Create Mental Pictures
Good readers picture what is happening in the story or text as they read.

Be a Problem-solver
When good readers cannot understand something, they take special steps to figure it out.

These seven strategies are used throughout the reading process. They include things you should do *before, during,* and *after* you read any reading selection. This chapter will look more closely at how these strategies work during each stage of the reading process.

BEFORE READING

When you are about to read something, you should always ask yourself:

★ *Why am I reading this selection?*

★ *What do I already know about this subject?*

Think about *why* you are reading the story or reading passage. For example, is it to find out specific information or to enjoy a good story? Next, try to get some general idea of what the reading is about by looking over the title and the text. See if there are illustrations, headings, or other clues about the subject of the reading. Then think about what you already know about that type of reading and its subject matter.

Finally, think of any questions you may have about the reading or its subject matter. What would you like to find out about that topic?

DURING READING

As you read, *make connections, ask questions,* and *make predictions.* You should also think about what is important and create mental images — pictures in the mind — as you read.

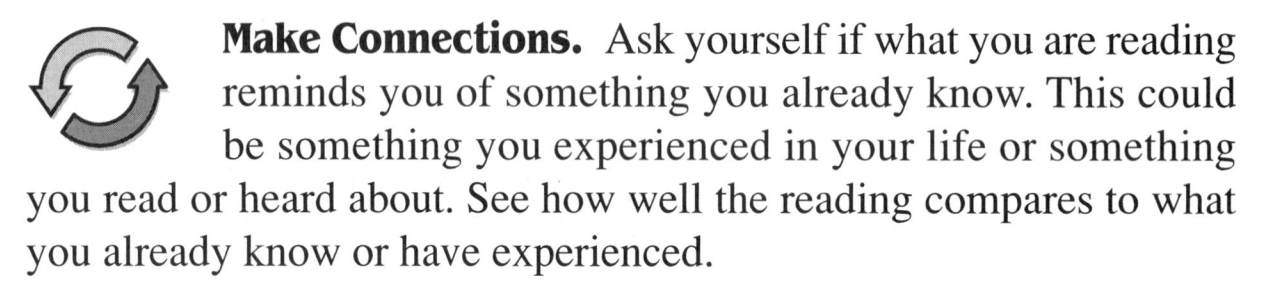

Make Connections. Ask yourself if what you are reading reminds you of something you already know. This could be something you experienced in your life or something you read or heard about. See how well the reading compares to what you already know or have experienced.

Ask Questions. Good readers ask questions about what they are reading. For example, good readers ask ***what*** is happening in the reading. They ask ***why*** things in the story happen the way they do. Asking questions helps you focus on what you are reading. You will learn more about asking questions later in this book.

Think about What Is Important. What is important in a reading will depend both on the reading itself and on your purpose for reading it. As you read, focus on the author's main ideas or key events in the story. As you read each detail, ask yourself if it is important to the overall meaning of the story or passage.

Often, important parts of the text will be identified for you. The title is important because it tells you what the passage is about. Headings, **bold** print, words in *italics* or in CAPITAL letters are usually important. Many paragraphs will have a **topic sentence** stating the main idea of the paragraph.

Create Mental Pictures. Much of what we know about the world comes from our five senses. Therefore, when you read, try to imagine the things you are reading about. For example, imagine you are listening as each story character speaks. Imagine what it would be like to smell, taste, or touch what a character is experiencing.

Make Predictions. Good readers make predictions about what what will come next. For example, if you are reading a story and the main character faces a problem, you might think about some of the ways the problem could be solved.

Summarize. Good readers often pause to think about what they have just read. They silently summarize in their own words what is important. They check details to make sure their summary is correct before they continue reading.

Be a Problem-Solver. When good readers have trouble understanding something, they take steps to figure it out. They may re-read a difficult section to make sure they understand it, or use clues to define difficult words.

AFTER READING

After you finish a reading, think about what you have just read. Think about what was **most important** in the reading. Mentally **summarize** what the reading was about. Think about what you learned from the reading, and how it fits in with what you already knew.

To become a good reader, you should ask yourself the following:

★ What was the message or main idea of the reading?

★ Have I learned something *new*?

★ What were some "memorable" words or phrases?

A SAMPLE MODEL

Let's see how a good reader uses these strategies with an actual reading. Read the passage below about the history of ice cream.

BEFORE READING

Before reading this passage, ask yourself:

> ★ *Why am I reading this selection?* I am reading this passage to find out how people first started eating ice cream, one of my favorite foods.
>
> ★ *What do I already know about this subject?* Today we make ice cream with freezers. I don't know how they made ice cream in earlier times.

DURING READING

Here are some of the things a good reader might be thinking about while reading this article on the history of ice cream.

MAKE CONNECTIONS
I already know what ice cream is. The title tells me I will learn some other "cool facts" about ice cream.

MAKE PREDICTIONS
From the text, I can tell this is an article, not a story. I predict the article will tell me more about the history of ice cream.

The Daily Journal

THE COLD FACTS ABOUT ICE CREAM
by Kristin Martelle

The first evidence of any kind of frozen sweets is from Alexander the Great in the fourth century B.C. Legend has it that this mighty leader enjoyed icy drinks. Once, he even had thirty trenches filled with snow to chill drinks for ladies' refreshment.

CREATE MENTAL PICTURES
I can just imagine Alexander's troops filling the trenches with snow in order to chill the drinks.

CHAPTER 1: HOW TO BE A GOOD READER

ASK QUESTIONS
As I read, I ask the following questions:
- ❏ What does *savor* mean?
- ❏ What else did Roman emperors want served at royal feasts?
- ❏ How did the Romans keep the snow from melting?
- ❏ Did Nero really execute the general?

> Roman emperors savored fruit pulps and juices flavored with honey and chilled with ice and snow. Emperor Nero demanded these "ices" be served at royal feasts. But getting snow from the faraway Alps was a challenge. Ways to keep the ice from melting were planned months in advance. Runners raced hundreds of miles to get their ice to Rome. Legend has it that once, when the snow melted before it reached Nero, he executed the general in command.

> By the year 1500, cream had been added to the recipes, and Italian nobles couldn't get enough "cream ice." The "cream ice" was brought to France in 1533 with the help of Catherine de Medici of Italy. When she married King Henry of France, she put her own chefs and dessert makers in the palace. For more than one hundred years the recipes were a closely guarded secret.

THINK ABOUT WHAT IS IMPORTANT
This paragraph seems important because it tells how iced drinks and cold desserts were turned into ice cream. As I read, I wonder why ice cream recipes were kept secret.

AFTER READING

After reading an article, the good reader thinks about what he or she has learned. Here, the reader learned about how ice cream developed in the past. After reading this article, the reader might:

★ add some new words — like *savor* — to his or her continuing list of vocabulary words;

★ create a graphic organizer of important information in the article;

★ write a summary of the main idea; or

★ go to the local library to take out books about ice cream.

CHAPTER 2

TOOLS FOR UNDERSTANDING UNFAMILIAR WORDS AND PHRASES

When you read, you may come across an unfamiliar word or phrase. This chapter introduces several tools you can use to figure out the meaning of an unfamiliar word or phrase.

USE WORD PATTERNS TO SOUND OUT THE WORD

The first step in figuring out a new word is sounding it out. By sounding out a word, you may find the unfamiliar word is one you already know. We use an alphabet of 26 letters to write out every sound in English. Because the English language has been influenced by other languages, the same sound is not always written in the same way. Even so, there are several different word patterns you should know. You have been learning these patterns ever since you started to read.

CONSONANT SOUNDS

Some sounds are made by blocking the flow of air with the throat, tongue, lips, or teeth. These are known as **consonant** sounds. The following letters are used for consonant sounds:

b c d f g h j k l m n p q r s t v w y z

Two special letters can make more than one consonant sound:

G can sound like a hard "g" [**g**ood] or a "j" [**g**eneral]

C can sound like "k" [**c**at] or a "s" [i**c**e]

Many words have *two or more consonant sounds* together. We blend these consonant sounds. Practice with these sounds.

blink   **pl**ay   **st**op

small   **spr**ing   **str**aw

Sometimes we use groups of consonant letters to make a special sound. Notice that these all use "*h.*"

sh	th	ch	tch
fish	think	church	watch

Now put in words with the same combinations:

Some special groups of consonants make a different sound than you might expect from their spelling.

ph = *f*	gh = *f*	kn = *n*	mb = *m*	wr = *r*	ght = *t*	sch = *sk*
phone	cough	know	lamb	write	right	school

Now put in words that use the same consonant groups and sounds:

VOWEL SOUNDS

Other sounds in English are known as vowel sounds. These sounds are made without blocking the flow of air as we speak. Five letters are used to make vowel sounds:

a e i o u

Each of these vowels can be *long* or *short*. When a vowel is long, it says its name. When a vowel is short, it makes a different sound.

Vowel	Long sound (¯)	Short sound (˘)
A	cāke	hăt
E	ēat	slĕd
I	hīke	hĭt
O	hōpe	hŏt
U	flūte	hŭt

To spell a long vowel sound, we often add another vowel, like *e* or *i*. The second vowel is usually silent. Often, the two vowels are separated by a consonant.

b**oa**t	s**oa**p	tr**ai**n	tr**ee**
g**at**e	r**op**e	f**in**e	l**ak**e

Remember this rule: when two vowels are together, the first one usually does the talking — says its name — and the second does the walking — stays silent.

Just as with consonants, certain groups of vowels make special sounds:

oo	**ou** or **ow**
b**oo**t	sh**ou**t / c**ow**

When you add "*r*" to a vowel or group of vowels, this also makes a special sound:

Can You Think of Another Word with that Sound?		
a	far	
e	were	
i	girl	
o	more	
u	cure	
ea	tear	
ai	fair	

Y is a special letter. It can act as both a *consonant* or a *vowel*:

consonant	vowel
yellow	bi**c**ycle

Sometimes the same combination of vowels can make different sounds:

ea	ou
m**ea**t st**ea**k	th**ou**ght sh**ou**t

Now practice sounding out the following words with your teacher, parent, or friend:

microscope	groom	photograph	swirl
disappoint	race	moose	bought
birch	fast	baseball	knight
tile	chirp	sidewalk	building

USE CONTEXT CLUES

Suppose you can sound out a word but you still do not know what the word means. The next step in figuring out the meaning of an unfamiliar word or phrase is to look at surrounding words and sentences.

These surrounding words and sentences often provide clues about the meaning of a word or phrase. The clues that surround a word or phrase are called **context clues.**

Sometimes the sentence or surrounding sentences will actually give you the definition. For example, read the following sentence:

> John saw Ms. Jones, the *superintendent*, who was in charge of all three of the town's elementary schools.

CHECKING YOUR UNDERSTANDING

What does the word *superintendent* mean? _____
_____

What context clue provides the hint? _____
_____

At other times, context clues may tell you what the unfamiliar word or phrase *is not*. Again, read the following sentence:

> Unlike the *idle* Mr. Adams, Ms. Smith was very busy every day.

CHAPTER 2: TOOLS FOR UNDERSTANDING UNFAMILIAR WORDS AND PHRASES   13

CHECKING YOUR UNDERSTANDING

What does the word *idle* mean? _____

_____

What context clue provides the hint? _____

_____

Often you will have to find clues throughout the passage to figure out the meaning of the unfamiliar word. Read the following passage:

> The athlete was *mammoth* in size. He was nearly seven feet tall. His arms were thicker than many people's legs. With his powerful and muscular arms, he could easily lift a car off the ground or throw a baseball out of the stadium.

CHECKING YOUR UNDERSTANDING

What does the word *mammoth* mean? _____

_____

What context clues provide the hint? _____

_____

14   MASTERING THE GRADE 3 ISAT READING AND WRITING TESTS

You could easily see the *irritated* expression on Jack's face at hearing the news. Jack was looking forward to seeing a movie with his mother. Just last week his mother had promised him they would go to the mall to see the new Disney movie. Now his mother had changed her mind. Instead, they would go shopping in the mall for school clothes.

CHECKING YOUR UNDERSTANDING

What does the word *irritated* mean? _____

_____

What context clue provides the hint? _____

_____

When you come across an unfamiliar word or phrase in a reading passage, think of yourself as a detective. Use context clues to figure out the meaning of the word or phrase. Let's summarize what we have just learned about using context clues:

★ Look at the other words in the sentence.

★ Read a few sentences **before** and **after** the sentence in which the unfamiliar word or phrase appears.

★ Based on the rest of the sentence and on neighboring sentences, try to guess the meaning of the word or phrase.

CHAPTER 2: TOOLS FOR UNDERSTANDING UNFAMILIAR WORDS AND PHRASES 15

> It may help to think of an unfamiliar word or phrase as an empty box. Based on what you read in the surrounding sentences, what word or words would you expect to find in that empty box?
>
> *In the cold climate of Scotland, many people enjoy hot ☐ for breakfast. They make their breakfast by boiling ground oats in hot water or milk.*
>
> What words do you think might fit in the box?
>
> • _____ • _____

USE YOUR KNOWLEDGE OF PARTS OF SPEECH

When you come across an unfamiliar word, it also helps if you can determine its **part of speech**. Most often, the unfamiliar word will be a *noun, verb, adjective,* or *adverb*.

★ A **noun** names a person, place, or thing.
   For example: ***Jack*** likes to play ***tennis.***

★ A **verb** is an *action* or *being* word — it tells what nouns do or what is being done to them.
   For example: He ***ate*** too much, and now he ***felt*** sick.

★ An **adjective** describes a noun.
   For example: I just bought a ***silver*** car.

★ An **adverb** describes a verb, adjective, or another adverb.
   For example: He ran ***very swiftly.***

Read the sentences below. After you read them, see if you can figure out what part of speech belongs in each blank box.

- ☐ is a very pretty girl.
- Tiffany ☐ her dinner.

Once you know the part of speech, it is easier to think of other words you might use in place of the unfamiliar word. The word you use to replace the difficult word should be the same part of speech.

USE WORD ANALYSIS

Another way to find the meaning of an unfamiliar word is to break it into parts. You can then see if any of these parts reminds you of other words you already know. First, divide the word into syllables. Each **syllable** is a word or part of a word pronounced with a single vowel sound. Some words have only one syllable, such as *hat*. Others have many syllables, such as *lol • li • pop*.

PREFIXES, ROOTS, AND SUFFIXES

Recognizing the syllables of a word can often help you to break down a word into smaller parts: *prefix, root,* and *suffix*. For example, let's look at the word *unbreakable*.

ROOTS

The *root* is the basic word to which prefixes and suffixes are added. In the word **unbreakable,** *break* is the **root.** Many common roots come from other languages. Which of these roots have you seen before — *astro* (space), *geo* (earth), *ped* (foot), *cycle* (wheel), *tele* (far), *scope* (to see), *aqua* (water), and *graph* (to write)?

PREFIXES

A **prefix** is a syllable or group of syllables added in front of the root to change its meaning. In the word **unbreakable,** *un* is the **prefix.** It changes the meaning of the entire word.

CHAPTER 2: TOOLS FOR UNDERSTANDING UNFAMILIAR WORDS AND PHRASES   17

Here are some common *prefixes* you may see while reading.

Prefix	Meaning	Examples
re	again	**re**view, **re**write
un	not	**un**happy, **un**healthy
mis	incorrectly	**mis**spell, **mis**lead
bi	two	**bi**cycle, **bi**annual
dis	not	**dis**comfort, **dis**like
pre	before	**pre**view, **pre**pay

Some prefixes can be confusing since they have more than one meaning. For example, *in* can mean *inside* (*indoors*) or *not* (*incorrect*).

SUFFIXES

A **suffix** is a syllable or group of syllables added to the end of a word. In the word **unbreakable,** *able* is the **suffix.** Now let's examine some common suffixes you will frequently see when reading.

Suffix	Meaning	Examples
ful	full of something	care**ful**, hope**ful**, trust**ful**
able	able to do something	break**able**, depend**able**
ness	state of being something	kind**ness**, happi**ness**, sad**ness**
er	person who does something	teach**er**, work**er**, carpent**er**
tion	state of doing something	ac**tion**, fascina**tion**, imita**tion**

When you analyze the word *unbreakable,* here is what we see:

un + **break** + **able**   *unbreakable* = not able to be broken

COMPOUND WORDS

A **compound word** is made up of two separate words that are added together to form a new word.

home + work = homework

By separating a compound word into its parts, you can often figure out what the word means. Try the examples that follow:

Word	What two words make up the compound word?	What does this word mean?
bodyguard	_____ + _____	
courtroom	_____ + _____	
everybody	_____ + _____	

If you break a difficult word into its parts, it can sometimes help you to figure out its meaning.

APPLYING WHAT YOU HAVE LEARNED

You should use *sounding out the word, context clues,* and *word analysis* to help you figure out the meaning of unfamiliar words.

- ❏ Try to sound out the word.
- ❏ Examine surrounding words and sentences for context clues.
- ❏ Figure out the part of speech of the unfamiliar word.
- ❏ Use word analysis by:
  - breaking the word into syllables
  - checking the word for familiar prefixes, roots, and suffixes
  - separating compound words into parts

CHAPTER 3

ADDITIONAL TOOLS FOR READING WITH UNDERSTANDING

In the previous two chapters you learned about the strategies used by good readers and some tools for word analysis. You are now ready to add two more tools to your "mental toolbox":

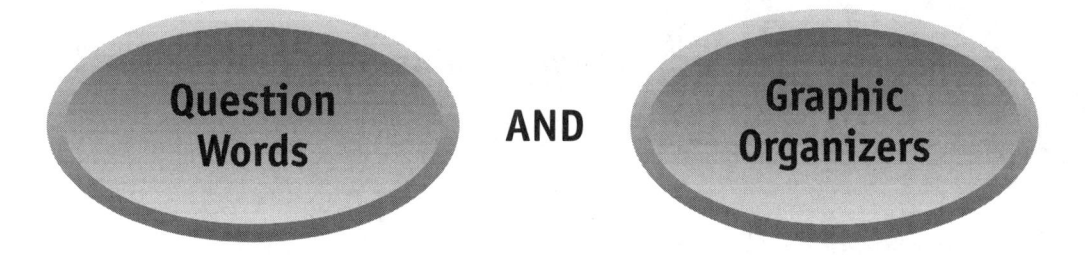

Question Words AND **Graphic Organizers**

Using these two tools will help you to better understand what you read and also to obtain your best score on the **Grade 3 ISAT Reading Test**.

USING QUESTION WORDS

In the first chapter, you learned that good readers ask questions. When news reporters are sent to cover a story, they want to find out what is happening. Reporters learn what is taking place by asking six basic questions:

WHAT? **WHO?** **WHEN?**

WHERE? **WHY?** **HOW?**

These words are known as the six **question words.** When you read a story or other type of reading, pretend you are a news reporter. Ask yourself as many of the six question words as you can:

WHAT QUESTIONS — *What* is happening in the story?

WHO QUESTIONS — *Who* are the main characters in the reading?

WHEN QUESTIONS — *When* is the story taking place?

WHERE QUESTIONS — *Where* is the story taking place?

CHAPTER 3: ADDITIONAL TOOLS FOR READING WITH UNDERSTANDING

WHY QUESTIONS — *Why* do the characters act as they do?

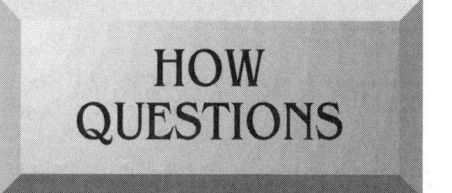

HOW QUESTIONS — *How* is this story going to end?

Whenever you read a story or any other type of reading, think about the six question words. Ask and answer these kinds of questions, and you will better understand what you have read.

Now read the passage below. It is the beginning of the book *The Courage of Sarah Noble* by Alice Dalgliesh.

NIGHT IN THE FOREST

Sarah lay on a quilt under a tree. The darkness was all around her, but through the branches she could see one bright star. It was comfortable to look at. The spring night was cold, and Sarah drew her warm cloak close. That was comfortable, too. She thought of how her mother had put it around her the day she and father started out on this long, hard journey.

CHECKING YOUR UNDERSTANDING

Now play the role of a news reporter. Write down as many questions about the story as you can. Use the six question words below as a guide. The first question word has been done for you.

WHAT?
- What did Sarah see through the branches?
- What did Sarah use to keep herself warm?

WHO?
- _____
- _____

WHEN?
- _____
- _____

WHERE?
- _____
- _____

WHY?
- _____
- _____

HOW?
- _____
- _____

CHAPTER 3: ADDITIONAL TOOLS FOR READING WITH UNDERSTANDING 23

USING GRAPHIC ORGANIZERS

Do you know what a graphic organizer is? A **graphic organizer** is a diagram that shows information. Often a graphic organizer uses circles, rectangles, and other shapes filled with important ideas and information. Sometimes, lines or arrows connect these shapes in order to show how one thing is related to another.

You can use a graphic organizer to identify information in a reading. Let's look at some of the ways graphic organizers help us to picture information.

TOPIC MAPS

One type of graphic organizer is a *topic map* or *web*. This is created by putting the topic or main idea of a reading in the center of the page. Then surround this topic or main idea with supporting facts and details. This type of graphic organizer is useful for a reading that *describes* an important idea, character, place, or event. Let's practice by reading the passage below. Then complete the topic map that follows.

THE HOUSE ON SANDLER'S LANE

Everyone in our community knew about the house at the end of Sandler's Lane. No one had lived in that dark, dreary house for more than a hundred years. Everyone knew that the house was haunted. Each Halloween, neighbors looked through the windows and swore they saw ghosts dancing inside the house. At other times of the year, people heard shrieks and other strange sounds coming from the house.

PRACTICE COMPLETING A TOPIC MAP

Directions: Fill in the blank boxes with details that help describe the house on Sandler's Lane. The first one has been done for you.

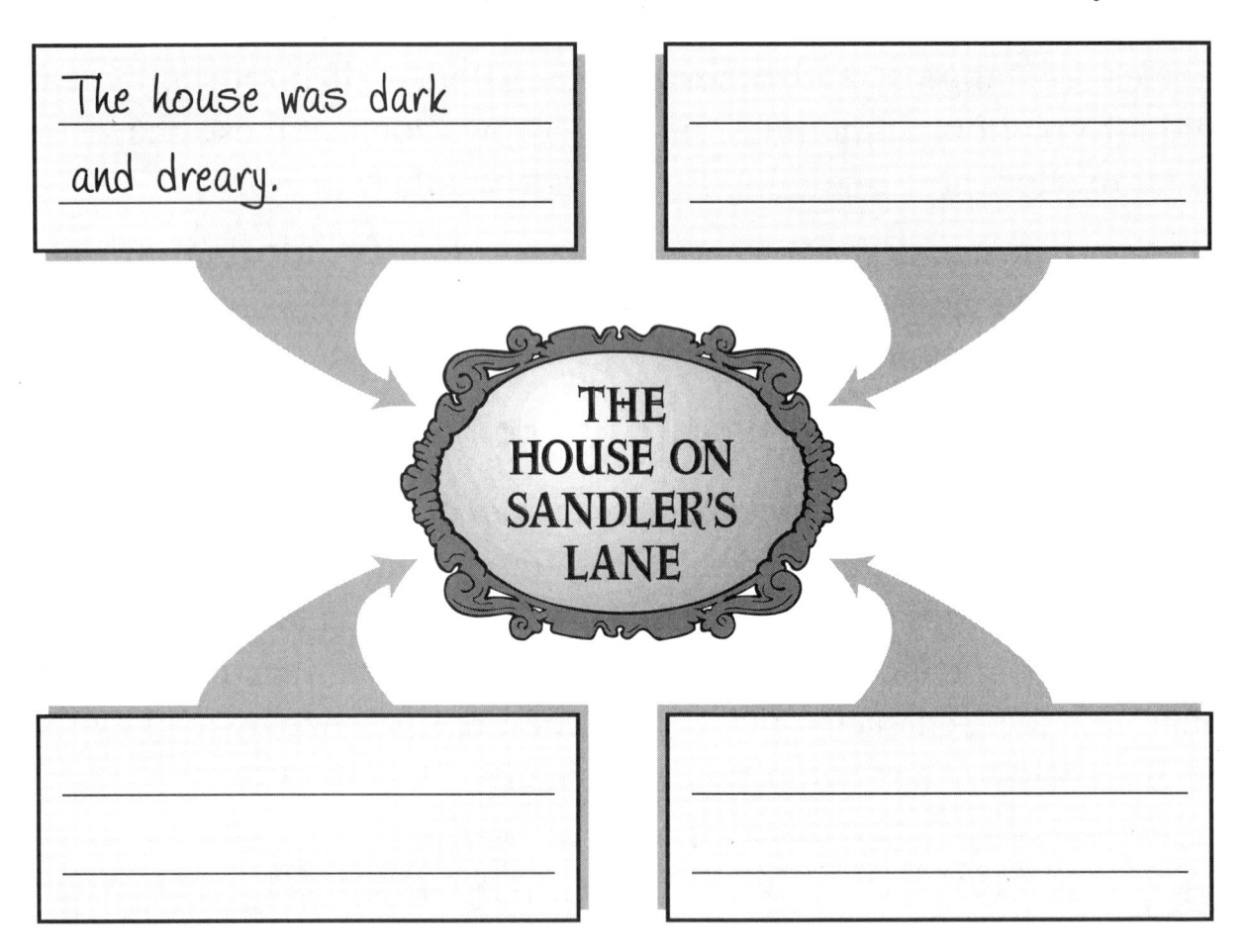

> The house was dark and dreary.

THE HOUSE ON SANDLER'S LANE

SEQUENCE MAPS

Many readings tell about a series of events. A **sequence map** can help you see how these events are related. They show how events in a story move from one event to the next. To make a sequence map, make a box or circle for each event in the order that the event occurred. Then connect these shapes by arrows to show the progress of events.

Read the story on the next page about a bold knight and a dragon. Then complete the sequence map that follows.

SIR GEORGE MEETS THE DRAGON

Sir George left his castle and set out on a very dangerous mission. A wicked dragon was burning villages and attacking innocent villagers. Sir George traveled for nearly two days, until suddenly his horse became frightened and stopped. The brave knight got off the horse. He put down his long lance. In the distance he saw a cave on the side of the mountain. Sir George could not see the monster, but he knew it was there. His nostrils filled with the smell of the dragon's fiery smoke, and his skin tingled from its heat.

Sir George, in full armor, began walking up the winding path that led to the dragon's cave. After the first turn, the dragon came into view. It was a bone-chilling sight. Taller than ten men, the dragon was covered with hard scales and breathed fire and smoke. Sir George ran straight up to the huge beast. An expression of surprise passed across the dragon's face as Sir George drove his sword into its body. The beast rose up and then slumped over. The terrifying dragon was dead!

PRACTICE COMPLETING A SEQUENCE MAP

Directions: Fill in the blank boxes on the following page to show the sequence of events in the story you just read. The first two boxes have been completed for you.

Sir George leaves his castle on a dangerous mission.

Sir George finds the dragon in its cave in the side of a mountain.

_____

_____

_____

VENN DIAGRAMS

A **Venn diagram** is another type of graphic organizer. It is used to compare and contrast two items, topics, or ideas. To make a Venn diagram, draw two ovals or other shapes, making sure the shapes overlap. In the overlapping area, write those things that the items have in common. In the parts of the ovals that do not overlap, write whatever is different about each item.

Now let's create a Venn diagram. First read the story that follows about Sally and Linda. Then complete the Venn diagram.

SALLY AND LINDA

Sally is the daughter of Linda. People say Linda and Sally have many features that are alike. Both have brown eyes and a pretty smile. They both sing the same quiet melody whenever they are happy. But Sally likes to sleep late, while her mother rises early in the morning. Linda enjoys eating at home, while Sally prefers eating in a restaurant.

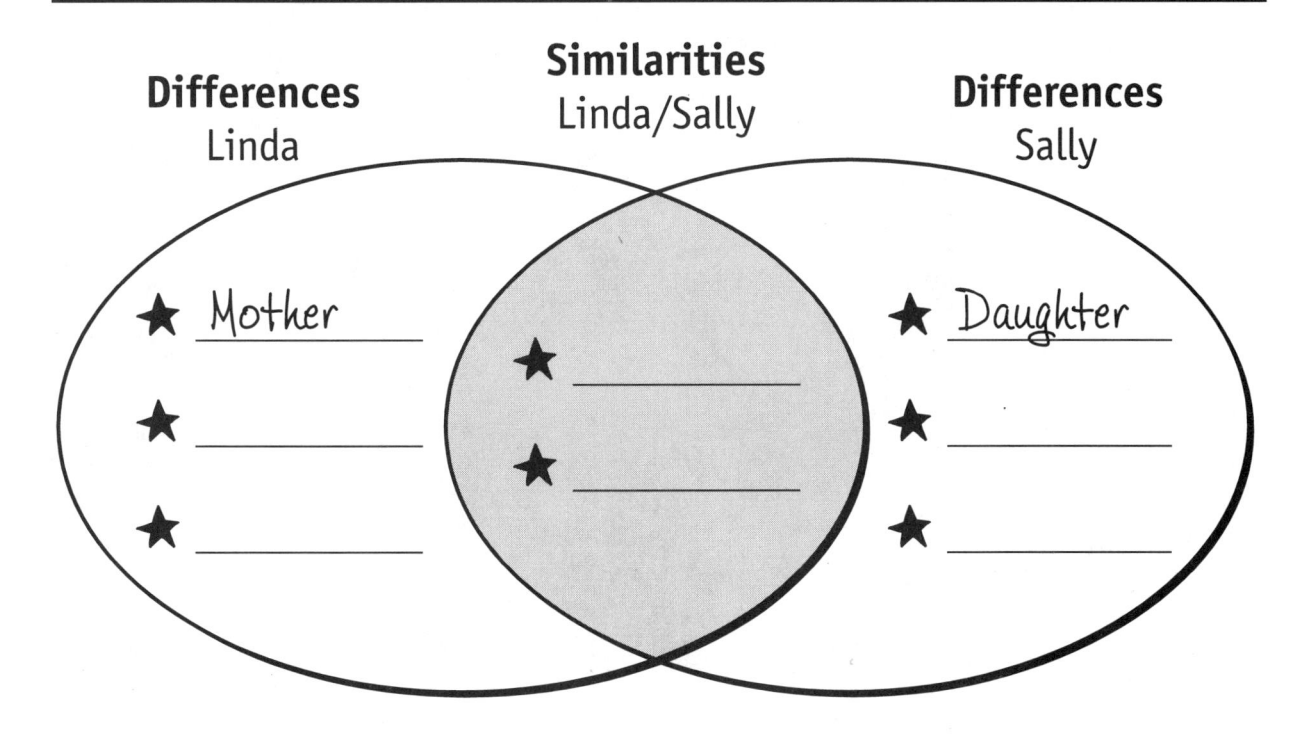

Differences — Linda | **Similarities** Linda/Sally | **Differences** — Sally

- ★ Mother
- ★ _____
- ★ _____

- ★ _____
- ★ _____

- ★ Daughter
- ★ _____
- ★ _____

Remember: You can make Venn diagrams using any kind of shape, including circles and rectangles.

You should use these three kinds of graphic organizers — *topic maps, sequence maps,* and *Venn diagrams* — to help you as you read and to keep track of different kinds of information. By showing how ideas, facts, or events are related, these charts will help you understand them better. As you read the rest of this book, you will see how these different types of graphic organizers can be used.

UNIT 2: TYPES OF READINGS

📕 **Chapter 4:** Reading Literary Texts

📕 **Chapter 5:** Reading Informational Texts

In this unit, you will learn about the types of readings that will be on the **Grade 3 ISAT Reading Test.** In general, the readings will be of two types:

★ **Literary Texts** are stories, legends, novels, and other works that we read for pleasure or to learn about the human experience. Most literary texts are fictional — they are about make-believe events.

★ **Informational Texts** include such things as articles, essays, histories, biographies, autobiographies and science. They are texts written about actual people, places, and things. We read informational texts to gain knowledge about something. Informational texts are also known as **nonfiction.**

Chapter 4

READING LITERARY TEXTS

There will be two main types of reading passages on the **Grade 3 ISAT Reading Test:** literary texts and informational texts. This chapter focuses on literary texts. A **literary text** is a fictional work, made up by the author. There are many types of literary texts, including stories, legends, and novels.

THE PARTS OF A STORY

There have been stories for as long as there have been people. The earliest stories were spoken. Storytellers told or sang myths and legends to groups of listeners. Later, stories were written down. Stories help explain how things happen in the world. By telling stories, we share our experiences with others.

We read stories and other forms of fiction for personal enjoyment. Good stories allow us to imagine what it would be like to live in faraway places or to have exciting adventures. We learn about people's experiences and lives. Stories also put us in touch with different human emotions. They can make us laugh or cry. They can make our hearts pound with excitement.

Do you have a favorite story? Why is it your favorite? What makes it such fun to read? Just as the recipe for a great dessert will contain many ingredients, so too does a good story.

If your favorite story is like most stories, it will have four main ingredients:

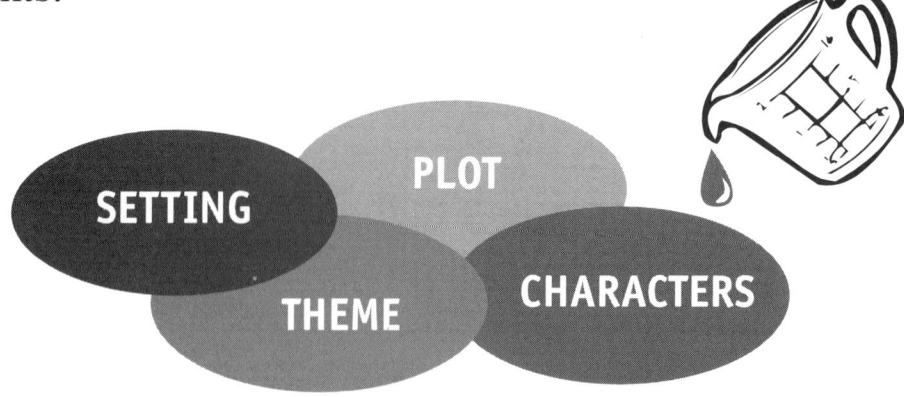

- SETTING
- PLOT
- THEME
- CHARACTERS

Do you know what each of these ingredients is? Let's look at a well-known story from ancient Greece to see how they blend together. As you read, remember to use the strategies of good readers — *ask questions, create mental images,* and *make predictions*. Use the sheet that follows the story to record your thoughts.

THE GOLDEN TOUCH

Long ago, in ancient Greece, a king named Midas spent much of his day eating and listening to music. One day, his gardener brought an old man to see him.

Midas immediately recognized the old man as Silenus. Midas knew Silenus was a close friend of Dionysus — the god of merry-making.

For ten days and nights, Midas entertained Silenus. Midas then brought Silenus back to Dionysus. Because Midas had entertained his friend Silenus, Dionysus was very happy.

CONTINUED

In return for this favor, Dionysus promised to grant Midas one wish. After some thought, Midas asked the god: "Would you grant that whatever I touch will turn immediately to gold?"

Dionysus gave Midas his wish. Soon after, Midas was delighted to find that a twig he touched immediately turned to gold. He picked up a stone, and it too turned to gold. When he reached his palace, he touched the doorway, and it too turned to gold. He was very excited by his new power.

By the time the sun set, Midas had grown tired of gold-making. He was hungry and thirsty. Midas ordered his servants to bring him food and drink. He tore off a piece of bread to satisfy his hunger. However, when he put it in his mouth he tasted cold metal. He then lifted his cup to drink, but his wine turned to liquid gold once it touched his lips.

Soon Midas was nearly dying from hunger and thirst. The sight of gold became hateful to him. He visited Dionysus to beg the god to take away the cursed golden touch. Dionysus took pity on Midas and let the king wash away the golden touch in a magical river.

When you read this story, did you ask questions and think about what you were reading? Answer the questions that follow. If needed, you may look back at the story.

BEING AN ACTIVE READER

1. What images come to mind when you visualize the old man Silenus? _____
_____
_____

2. How does the story remind you of anything you have done already or knew about? _____
_____
_____
_____

3. What questions do you have about the story? _____
_____
_____
_____

4. What words or phrases from the reading would you like to make part of your everyday vocabulary? _____
_____
_____

Let's take a closer look at each of the different "ingredients" of the story: *setting, characters, plot,* and *theme.*

THE STORY SETTING

The story setting is **when** and **where** the story takes place. Often the setting is described at the beginning of the story. Sometimes the author gives clues to indicate the story's time and place. You must examine the clues in the story to figure out the time and place.

A story setting can be in the past, present, or future, or even in an imaginary world where time hardly seems to exist. Fairy tales often begin with "Once upon a time …" to indicate an imaginary setting. A long story may even have more than one setting. As you read, try to create *mental images* of where the story takes place.

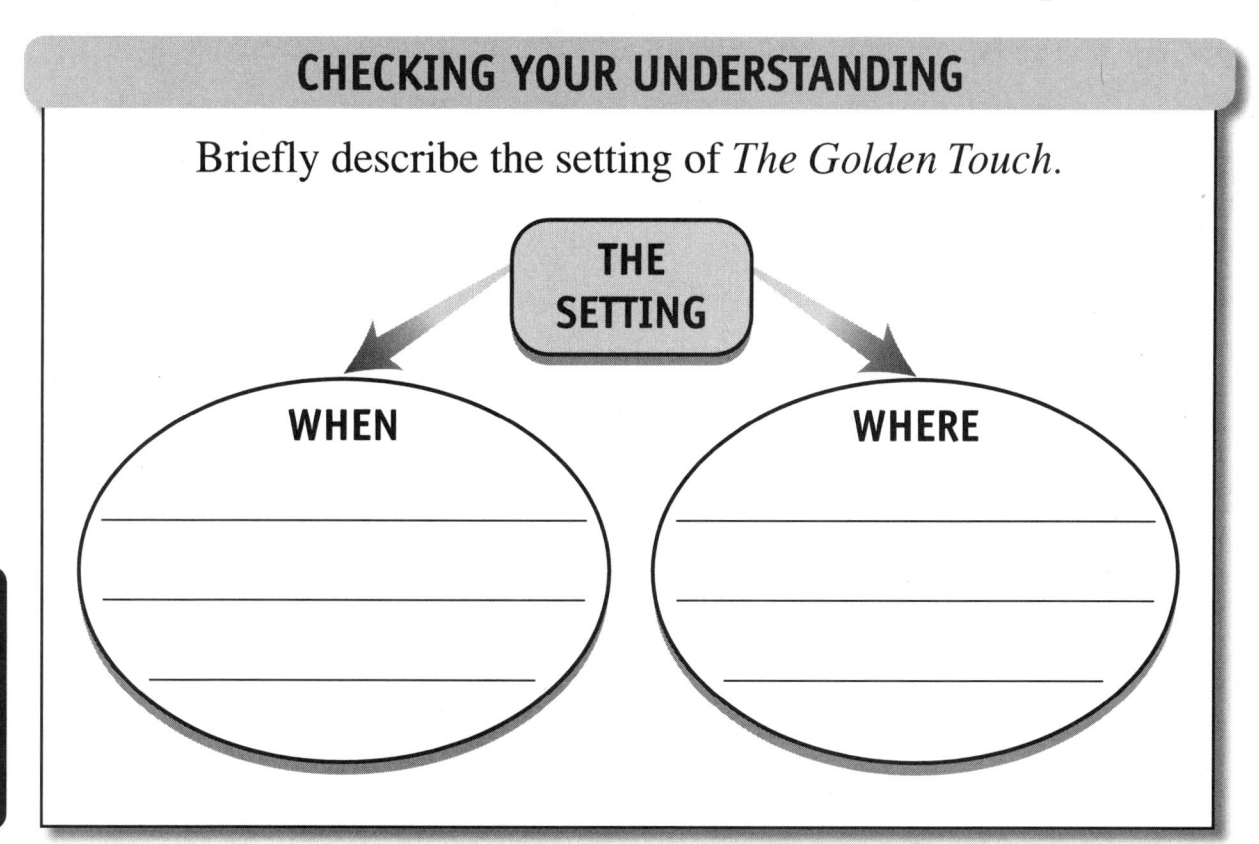

CHECKING YOUR UNDERSTANDING

Briefly describe the setting of *The Golden Touch*.

THE SETTING

WHEN
_____
_____
_____

WHERE
_____
_____
_____

THE STORY CHARACTERS

The characters of a story are *who* the story is about. Characters can be imaginary people or real people in an imaginary setting. Story characters may even be animals or objects that act like people. In **fables,** a special type of story, the main characters are often animals.

Most stories have only one or two main characters. Although a story may have several other characters, these other characters are less important.

The story is mostly about the main characters and their adventures. Readers identify with the main characters by imagining what it would be like to be them. Sometimes the author will describe what a character is like by creating a picture of that character with words. At other times, you have to figure out what the characters are like by the way they act and what they do in the story.

When reading or listening to a story, you should ask yourself the following questions about the characters:

★ What do they look like?

★ How do they act?

★ What do they think and feel?

★ How do they change as the story develops?

CHAPTER 4: READING LITERARY TEXTS   35

CHECKING YOUR UNDERSTANDING

List the characters in *The Golden Touch*.

(1) _____   (3) _____

(2) _____   (4) _____

Who is the main character of the story? _____

Complete a topic map describing the main character of the story.

THE STORY PLOT

The plot is **what happens** in the story. In most stories, the main characters face one or more problems. Sometimes a character wants to do something that is difficult, like climb a mountain or win a race. At other times, the main character has a conflict with another character in the story. For example, two boys may be competing with each other for the top prize in a contest.

The **plot** is the series of events that unfold in the story. As these events take place, the characters try to solve or overcome the main problem they face in the story. As you read or listen to a story, try to focus on the *most important* events in the plot.

An author often tries to maintain the reader's interest by creating some kind of excitement and suspense. The reader wants to continue reading the story to find out what happens.

As the plot unfolds, new twists or unexpected turns often occur, making the main problem worse. Eventually, the main characters think of a way to solve their problems or learn to accept them.

When you are reading or listening to a story, you should ask these questions about the plot:

★ What problems do the main characters face?

★ What events in the story affect these problems?

★ What actions do the characters take to deal with these problems?

★ Are the problems finally solved? If so, how are they solved?

CHECKING YOUR UNDERSTANDING

It often helps to make a sequence map to follow the plot of a story. Complete the sequence map below for *The Golden Touch*. Only include the most important events. The first two events have been completed for you:

| The palace gardener brings an old man before King Midas. | → | Midas knows the man as a friend of the god Dionysus and entertains him. |

↓

[_____]

↓

| | → | | → | |

Another way you can make a sequence map is by drawing pictures. Pretend you are creating a comic book of the story, *The Golden Touch*. Make a comic strip showing the main events. Remember, it is *not* your artistic ability that is important, but how well you show the story. Use a separate sheet of paper to create your comic strip.

THE STORY THEME OR LESSON

Stories usually teach us a message or lesson we can use in our own lives. This *message* or *lesson* is often called the **theme** of the story. Some stories have more than one theme. Themes show and tell us about life and human nature.

This is true of the story you read, *The Golden Touch*. One lesson of that story is that it often pays to help others. Remember that King Midas entertained the old man Silenus. In return for being nice to him, Midas was granted one wish by the god Dionysus.

CHECKING YOUR UNDERSTANDING

1. Briefly describe another theme or lesson of *The Golden Touch*. It may help you to recall what happened when Midas got his wish.

   _____
   _____
   _____
   _____

2. In what way does a theme of the story remind you of anything that has happened in your own life or that you have read or learned about? Explain.

   _____
   _____
   _____
   _____

Practice Exercises

Directions: Read the story below by Pleasant DeSpain. Then complete the graphic organizer that follows:

OLD JOE AND THE CARPENTER

Old Joe lived in the country by himself. His best friend was his closest neighbor. They had grown old together. Their wives had died, and their children were grown and had moved away. All they had left were their farms and each other.

For the first time in their long friendship, they had a disagreement. It was a silly argument over a stray calf that neither one of them really needed. The calf was found on Old Joe's neighbor's land, and he claimed it.

Old Joe said, "No, that calf has the same marking as one of my cows, and it belongs to me!"

They were stubborn men, and neither would give in. Rather than hit each other, they stopped talking. They stomped off to their respective homes. Two weeks went by without a word between them.

One Saturday morning, Old Joe heard a knock on his door. He was surprised to find a young man who called himself a "carpenter" standing on his porch. He had a toolbox at his feet, and there was kindness in his eyes. "I'm looking for work," he explained. "If you have a project, I'd like to help out."

CONTINUED

Old Joe replied, "As a matter of fact, I do have a job for you. See that house there? It's my neighbor's. You see that creek along our property line? That creek wasn't there last week. He did that to spite me! He dug that creek-bed from the pond right down the property line and then flooded it. Now that creek separates us. I'm so mad at him! I've got lumber in my barn and everything you'll need to build a tall fence all along that creek. Then I won't have to see his place any more. That'll teach him!"

The carpenter smiled and said, "I will do a good job for you, Joe."

The old man had to go to town for supplies. He got on his wagon and left. The young carpenter carried the lumber from the barn to the creek and started to work. He measured, sawed, and nailed the boards into place all day without stopping. With the setting of the sun, he went to put his tools away. He was finished.

Old Joe pulled up, his wagon filled with supplies. When he saw what the carpenter had built, he couldn't speak. It wasn't a fence, but a beautiful footbridge that reached from one side of the creek to another.

Just then, Old Joe's neighbor crossed the bridge, his hand stuck out, and said, "I'm sorry about our argument, Joe. The calf is yours, I just want us to be friends."

"You keep the calf," Old Joe said. "I want us to be friends, too. The bridge was this young fellow's idea. And I am glad he did it."

CHAPTER 4: READING LITERARY TEXTS   41

One way to understand what you have read is to create an outline. Complete the outline below on the story you just read. It will help you organize ideas from the story.

STORY OUTLINE

TITLE: _____

SETTING: _____

★ Where: _____

★ When: _____

MAIN CHARACTERS: ★ Who: _____

★ Who: _____

★ Who: _____

PLOT: *(List the events in the order that they happened)*

❶ _____

❷ _____

❸ _____

❹ _____

THEME OR LESSON: _____

_____

"GOOD READER" IDEAS: List questions about the reading or connections with what you already know.

_____

CHAPTER 5

READING INFORMATIONAL TEXTS

A second type of passage you will find on the **Grade 3 ISAT Reading Test** is an informational reading.

TYPES OF INFORMATIONAL READINGS

Informational readings, called **nonfiction,** are about real people, places, events, and things. They come in a wide variety of forms.

★ **Articles.** Articles are short informational pieces that are usually read in one sitting. You can find articles in newspapers, magazines, and encyclopedias. They tell you the basic facts about something. Let's examine the beginning of a typical article from a newspaper.

Mapletown News

LIGHTNING STRIKES HOUSE ON TAYLOR STREET

At 11:30 p.m. last night, a home on Taylor Street was hit by lighting during a violent thunderstorm. No one was injured.

Mr. Jones, owner of the home at 42 Taylor Street said, "We were all asleep when we were suddenly awakened by this very loud noise."

The purpose of an article is generally to tell a reader the *who, what, when, where, why,* and *how* of something. *Does this article tell the reader something about each of these question words?*

★ **Essays.** An **essay** gives an author's opinions and feelings about a single topic or issue. Let's look at an essay about cats.

THIS MAN'S BEST FRIEND — CATS

Of all the world's creatures, I have to admit that I admire cats the most. Ever since I was a young boy growing up in Springfield, there was just something about the sleek bodies, pointed ears, whiskers, and eyes of cats that inspired instant love in me. When a cat gently purrs and rubs its body against my leg, it establishes a place of love in my heart.

> In this essay, the author gives his feelings about cats and their impact on his life.
> *How does the author feel about cats?*

★ **Biography/Autobiography.** A **biography** is an article or book written by someone about a person's life and accomplishments. An **autobiography** is an article or book in which someone writes about his or her own life.

CLEOPATRA
by Haydon Middleton

Two thousand years ago, the king of Egypt had a baby daughter. Her name was Cleopatra. Cleopatra's family had ruled Egypt for 300 years, but they themselves were not Egyptians. The family had come from Greece. They spoke Greek, not Egyptian. They worshipped Greek gods and goddesses.

> This biography tells the story of the life of Cleopatra, Queen of ancient Egypt. This example is just the first paragraph of an entire book.
> *How can you tell that the information in this passage is from a biography and not an autobiography?*

All of these types of readings have something in common. They give information about a topic. The title and the first paragraph of each reading usually identifies the topic of the reading. The **topic** is the subject of the reading — what it is mostly about.

> **The following passage is the beginning of a longer article. Read the passage. Then identify the topic of the article.**

TREASURE HUNTER
by Ellen Hobart

Inch by inch, wiggle by wiggle, something down there is moving. It creeps along the sandy ocean floor. It moves past the swaying seaweed and around the rusty anchor chain.

It's the carrier snail, and it's hunting for treasure. Right now, it might be looking for a small skinny shell. Later on, it might choose a smooth speckled stone or a jagged piece of coral. The snail is always searching for the perfect piece to add to its collection.

CHECKING YOUR UNDERSTANDING

1. What is the topic of this article? _____

2. What are some things you would expect to learn from this article? _____
_____

CHAPTER 5: READING INFORMATIONAL TEXTS   45

THE PARTS OF AN INFORMATIONAL READING

Just as stories have different parts, so do informational readings. There are two major parts to an informational reading:

The MAIN Idea

SUPPORTING DETAILS

Do you know how each part works? Let's look at a short informational reading. As you read this passage, remember to use the strategies of good readers — *ask questions, create mental pictures,* and *make predictions.* Use the data sheet that follows to record your thoughts.

ABRAHAM LINCOLN

Abraham Lincoln was one of our greatest Presidents. When he was elected in 1860, slavery was permitted in much of the United States. Southern states feared Lincoln would end slavery. They tried to set up their own separate country. Lincoln led Americans into the Civil War to reunite the country. He bravely kept fighting despite many battlefield losses. Victory in the war finally reunited the country and ended slavery.

Abraham Lincoln

Library of Congress

You may wish to look back at this reading about Abraham Lincoln as you answer the following questions:

BEING AN ACTIVE READER

1. What did you already know about the subject of the reading?

2. What information in the reading did you find interesting?

3. What questions did you have about the reading?

4. What did you think was important in the reading?

5. What new words or phrases from the reading would you like to make a part of your everyday vocabulary?

THE MAIN IDEA OF A READING

The general point that an author makes about the topic of a reading is known as the **main idea.** For example, an author may show you that the subject of a biography was a very good person by telling you about her good deeds. Or the author may show that a place is very dangerous by pointing out the dangers experienced by visitors.

Remember, the *main idea* is not any particular detail. It describes what the reading is about *as a whole.* It is the most important thing in the reading.

FINDING THE MAIN IDEA

When you read something for information, you can take two steps to find the main idea.

> **STEP 1:**
> Decide the topic of the reading.

Determine the general subject of the reading. Is it about a person, place, idea, or event? Think of the topic as an umbrella. It should be large enough to cover everything discussed in the reading. For example, the topic of the reading on page 45 was **Abraham Lincoln.**

> **STEP 2:**
> See what the writer is saying overall about the topic.

Once you have decided on the topic, focus on what the writer has to say about it. Look for an overall message about the topic. This message is the author's main idea. Other details in the reading should explain or support this message.

Sometimes a special sentence in the reading will identify the main idea. Often it is at the beginning or end of the reading. At other times the main idea is unstated. The reader has to figure it out from the details.

In the paragraph on Abraham Lincoln, the main idea was that Lincoln was one of our nation's greatest Presidents. The specific facts mentioned in the reading help to support this main idea.

CHECKING YOUR UNDERSTANDING

Identifying the Main Idea. Imagine that this list of points was made in an informational reading. Check (✔) the one point that states the main idea of the informational reading.

- ☐ Apples are good for the lungs.
- ☐ Blueberries help to slow down the body's aging process.
- ☐ Eating fruit helps to keep the body healthy.
- ☐ Oranges provide the body with Vitamin C.

Explain your choice: _____

_____

As you learned in this chapter, the *topic* and *main idea* of an informational reading are often identified *early* in the reading. The author tells readers what the reading is about.

You can also check the *end* of the reading. Sometimes, the conclusion will summarize the main idea and review the most important details in the passage. Also examine the title, subheadings, and illustration captions for clues to the main idea.

THE SUPPORTING DETAILS

To help the reader understand the main idea or to show the reader that the main idea is correct, an author supplies examples, details, and illustrations. Each of these helps to support the author's main idea. It is through the use of these details and examples that the author explains the main idea and tries to show that it is correct.

CHECKING YOUR UNDERSTANDING

What were some of the details used by the writer to support the idea that Abraham Lincoln was a great President?

★ _____
_____

★ _____
_____

★ _____
_____

CHANGING WHAT YOU HAVE READ INTO A GRAPHIC ORGANIZER

It is sometimes easier to understand the main idea and supporting details of a reading by looking at a graphic organizer. You learned about graphic organizers in **Chapter 3.** Let's see how the paragraph about Abraham Lincoln might be turned into a graphic organizer. Does this diagram help you see the relationship between the main idea and supporting details?

Main Idea

Abraham Lincoln was one of our greatest Presidents.

- Lincoln led Americans into the Civil War to reunite the country.
- He bravely kept fighting despite many battlefield losses.
- Victory in the war reunited the country and ended slavery.

Supporting Details

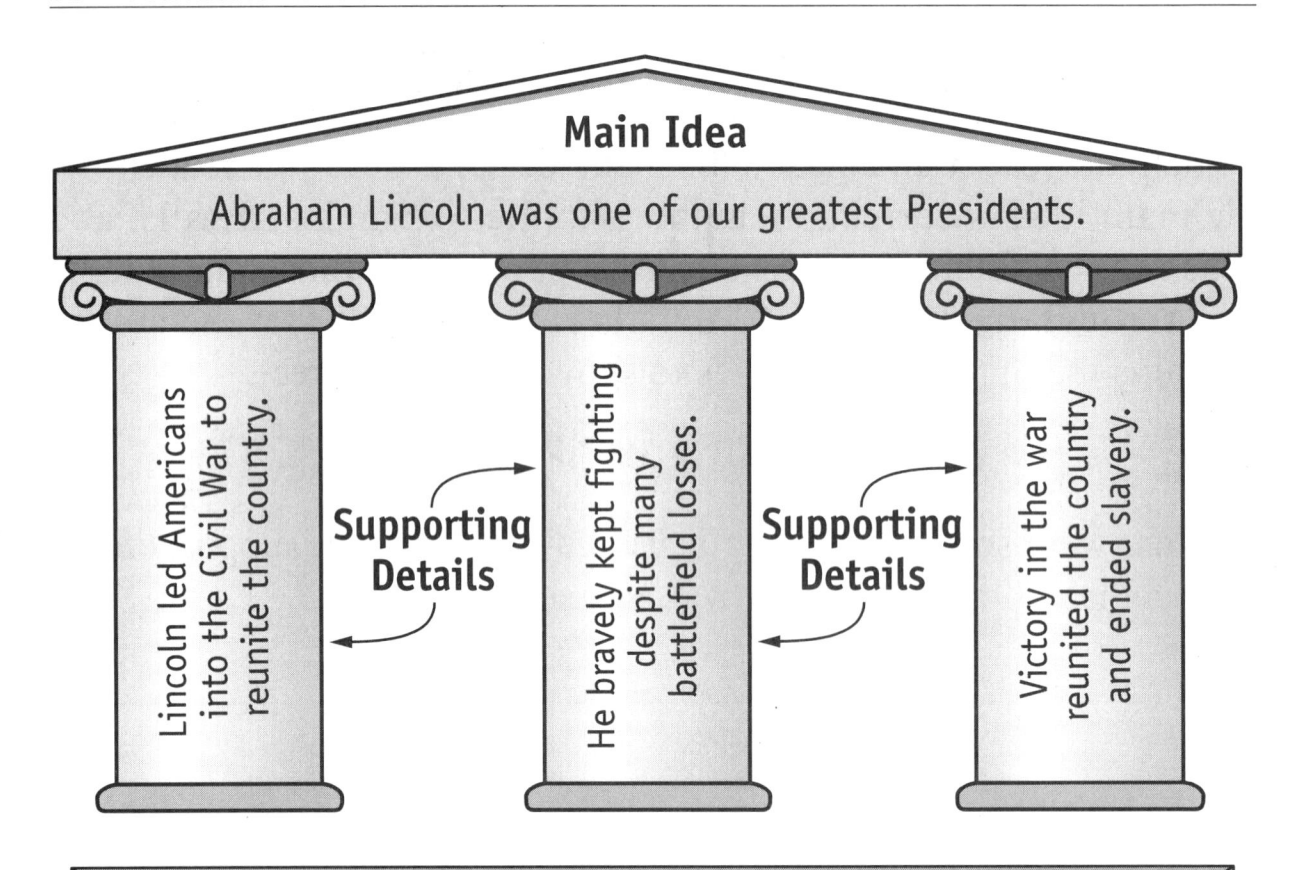

SUMMARY: TYPES OF READING

In Chapters 3 and 4, you learned about two different types of readings. Remember that what you find in a reading will depend largely on the type of reading it is.

IN A LITERARY TEXT

In a literary text, you can expect to find a setting, characters, and a plot. In addition, you can expect to find one or more themes.

IN AN INFORMATIONAL READING

In an informational reading, you can expect to find a topic, a main idea about that topic, and supporting details. Supporting details may include descriptions, facts, and examples.

Practice Exercises

Directions: Read the following paragraph from "Treasure Hunter" by Ellen Hobart. Then identify the topic, main idea, and the supporting details or examples.

> Animals often have special ways of protecting themselves from enemies. Many animals use their color to help keep them safe. It is one of nature's built-in protections. The brown sparrow looks like part of the nest it sits upon. The winter coats of some jackrabbits match the color of the winter's snow. The spotted fish blends in with the pebbles of the mountain stream that it swims in.

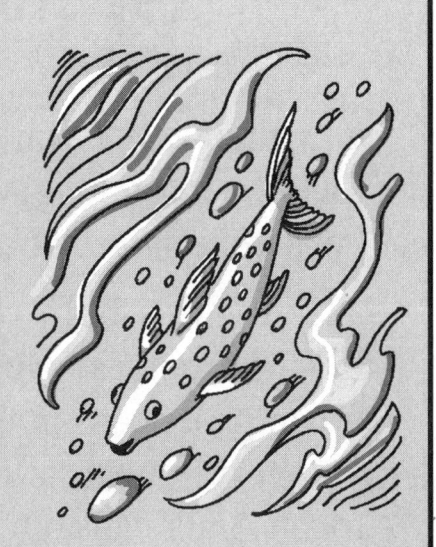

CHECKING YOUR UNDERSTANDING

1. What is the *topic* of this paragraph? _____

2. What is the *main idea* of this paragraph? _____

3. List *three* supporting details from the paragraph:

   ★ _____
   ★ _____
   ★ _____

Directions: Read the following article about a young African American's experiences at West Point — a school where cadets learn to become officers in the U.S. Army. Then identify the *main idea* and the most important *supporting details* in a graphic organizer.

THE STORY OF HENRY FLIPPER
by Bea Bragg

As the West Point ferry docked, seventeen-year old Henry Flipper, a young African American, tugged at his shirtsleeves. *How will I do at the U.S. Military Academy at West Point?*

Henry was born of slave parents in 1856 in Georgia. Until the Civil War, African Americans in the South were kept in slavery. Even after the Civil War, African Americans often faced prejudice.

After the war ended in 1865, Henry received an education in schools run by Northern sympathizers. He was confident his teachers had prepared him well for West Point. He was not so confident about how he would put up with the insults that other black men had received there. If he fought back, would he lose everything he had dreamed of — becoming an engineer and a proud soldier?

As Henry walked past the barracks on his first day, cadets leaned from windows, teasing and jeering him. Henry, who was more than six feet tall, pulled himself up, looked straight ahead, and walked on.

Henry faced isolation and loneliness at West Point, but did well academically. He had never felt such joy as when he successfully completed all of his exams. "I was so happy. The other cadets shook my hand. All signs of prejudice were gone."

CONTINUED

On June 14, 1877 graduates received their diplomas. When Henry's name was called, a roar went up from the audience. The roar drowned out the pounding in Henry's ears. They were applauding him. Fellow cadets crowded around him to shake his hand.

Henry was the first black graduate of West Point. He was assigned to Fort Sill in Oklahoma. At this post, he received praise for designing a ditch that drained water from the area, eliminating malaria — a serious health problem.

Student cadets practice marching at West Point.

Henry was happy at Fort Sill. Things changed when he was transferred to Fort Davis in Texas. There, a superior officer charged him with stealing and "conduct unbecoming an officer and a gentleman." Henry was cleared of the stealing charge, but was dismissed from the army. He was broken-hearted. For the rest of his life, he tried to have his dismissal reversed.

Henry went on to become a famous engineer, whose skill gained him national and international fame. He also served as a newspaper editor, translator, scholar, writer, and historian.

Henry Flipper died in 1940 at the age of 84. Forty years later the army cleared his name. In 1978, his remains were taken from a grave in Atlanta and moved to his home town. He was reburied with full military honors.

CONTINUED

54 MASTERING THE GRADE 3 ISAT READING AND WRITING TESTS

> In 1977, one hundred years after Henry's graduation, an award in his name was established at West Point. It was to be given to "the cadet who demonstrated the highest qualities of leadership and determination in the face of unusual difficulties." Henry Flipper would have been so proud!

Now that you have completed reading the article, fill in the graphic organizer below. It has already been started for you.

MAIN IDEA: Although Henry Flipper faced many obstacles in his life, he achieved many successes.

SUPPORTING DETAIL: Henry became the first African American to graduate from West Point.

SUPPORTING DETAIL: _____

SUPPORTING DETAIL: _____

UNIT 3: QUESTIONS ON THE READING TEST

- **Chapter 6:** Questions on Opening Impressions
- **Chapter 7:** Questions on Vocabulary and Word Analysis
- **Chapter 8:** Questions about Details in a Reading
- **Chapter 9:** Questions about Connections between Details
- **Chapter 10:** Questions on the Main Idea or Theme
- **Chapter 11:** Answering Extended-Response Questions
- **Chapter 12:** Testing Your Understanding

> The **Grade 3 ISAT Reading Test** usually has about 65 multiple-choice questions and two or three extended-response questions. In this unit, you will learn about the different kinds of multiple-choice and extended-response questions on the test and how to answer them.

INTRODUCTION TO ANSWERING MULTIPLE-CHOICE QUESTIONS

The **Grade 3 ISAT Reading Test** will have multiple-choice questions about each passage you read. A **multiple-choice question** is a question followed by several possible answers. Your job is to pick the choice that best answers the question. Here is an example:

---

1. How many hours are there in one day?
  A   7 hours
  B   12 hours
  C   24 hours
  D   48 hours

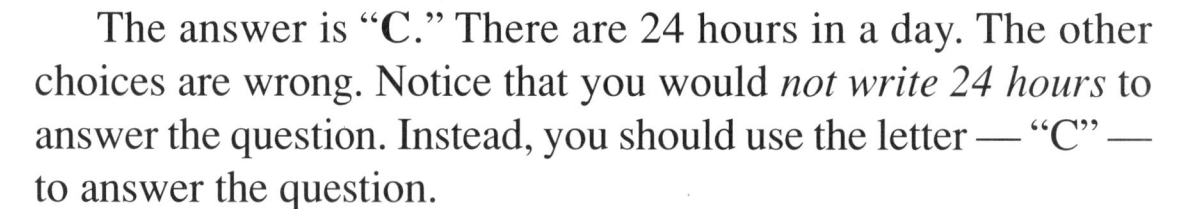

The answer is "C." There are 24 hours in a day. The other choices are wrong. Notice that you would *not write 24 hours* to answer the question. Instead, you should use the letter — "C" — to answer the question.

On the test, each multiple-choice question will be followed by four possible answers. Most of these questions will test your understanding of a reading passage. Some special questions on the test will test your ability in word analysis, including your understanding of the sounds of written words.

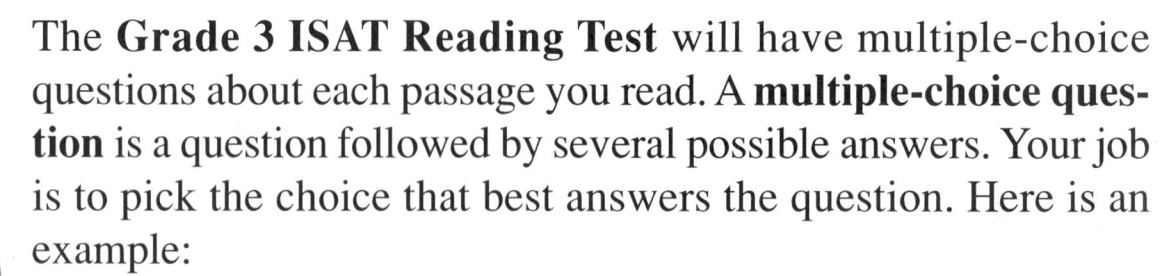

Multiple-choice questions about a reading fall into five main types. Each type of question focuses on a different step of the reading process:

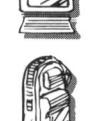

1. **Get a general impression of what the reading is about**

2. **Figure out the meaning of unfamiliar words or phrases**

3. **Focus on details in the reading:** *who, what, when,* and *where*

4. **See how details are connected: think about** *how* **and** *why*

5. **See how details in the reading lead to a** *main idea* **or** *theme*

In a sense, questions about a reading are arranged as if you were approaching the reading from a distance.

★ At first, you can see only roughly what the reading is about. You get a first impression about the reading.

★ Then you look at the reading more closely. You start to see the different parts of the reading passage. You start to focus on those parts and how they are connected.

★ When you are done looking at the parts, you step back again to view the reading as a whole (*to see what the whole reading is about*).

Multiple-choice questions can test your ability to understand the reading at each of these steps. The next five chapters in this unit will introduce you to each of these types of questions and show you how to answer them.

CHAPTER 6

QUESTIONS ON OPENING IMPRESSIONS

On the **Grade 3 ISAT Reading Test,** one of the first questions you are likely to see about any reading passage will ask you for your general impressions. This type of multiple-choice question will often appear in the following ways:

> ★ What is the reading passage mostly about?
>
> ★ What would be the best title for this reading passage?

To answer this kind of multiple-choice question, first read the passage carefully. Then think about what you have read. What was the most important information in the reading?

LITERARY TEXTS

In a literary text, think about the main characters, the central problem, and the most important events in the story. Try to make up a sentence in your head that summarizes what happened in the story.

The Golden Touch, for example, was a story about a king who was given the power to turn everything he touched into gold. The king soon found out that this was not what he really wanted in life.

INFORMATIONAL TEXTS

An informational reading is somewhat different from a story. In an informational reading, the question asks you about the main subject matter or topic of the reading.

In the article about Henry Flipper, you read about a young African American. You learned how he attempted to overcome the prejudice he faced as a student at West Point. The topic of the article was the life of Henry Flipper.

Remember that the *topic* of an informational reading will often be stated at the beginning of the passage. Look at the title and any sub-headings in the reading for clues.

At other times, the topic will not be stated. Use details in the reading to figure it out. Ask yourself — *what do the details in this reading have in common?*

After you form a general impression of the reading, look over the answer choices. Select the answer that best summarizes the whole reading. Choices that focus on individual details rather than the whole story or reading are probably not the correct answer.

If you are not sure which answer is best, review the passage a second time by **skimming.** To skim, read the passage over quickly to get a general sense of what it is all about.

Let's practice answering questions that ask what an informational reading is *mostly about*. Read the passage on the next page. Then answer the question that follows.

It looks easy! Glancing around a Chinese or Japanese restaurant, you see diners using chopsticks with ease. But when *you* try handling the long wooden utensils, one chopstick crosses over the other, and your food plops back onto your plate. In desperation, you spike a shrimp with the pointed end of a chopstick. The food makes it to your mouth. But to the Japanese, what you just did is as rude as eating peas with a knife.

Why did anyone ever think eating with wooden sticks was a good idea? Well, it was better than eating with your fingers, which is what most people did five thousand years ago.

A Chinese story explains that once, a hungry person couldn't wait for his food to cool. He grabbed a couple of sticks, and pulled out a piece of meat. The others copied him. The use of chopsticks soon spread to other Asian countries and reached Japan by about 500 A.D.

1. What would be the best title for this reading selection?
   A Restaurant Food
   B The Story of Chopsticks
   C Dining in Japan
   D A Hungry Person

CHECKING YOUR UNDERSTANDING

What is the answer to **Question 1**? _____ Explain your choice.

_____

Now let's practice answering an *opening impression question* about a story. Read the story. Then answer the question that follows.

> A lion slept in the forest. A mouse ran across the lion's nose. Awakened, the lion grabbed the tiny creature. The poor mouse begged, "Please, please, spare me. Let me go and one day I'll repay you." The lion was amused to think a mouse could ever help him. Being a generous lion, he let the mouse go.
>
> Some days later, the lion was caught in a hunter's net. Unable to free himself, the lion roared angrily. The mouse knew his voice and ran to help the lion. Jumping onto the ropes of the hunter's net, the little mouse began to chew at them. Before long the lion was free.
>
> "You laughed when I said I would repay you," said the mouse. "Now you see that even a little mouse can help a huge lion."

2. What is the story mostly about?
   A A little mouse who is almost eaten by a lion.
   B A little mouse who can eat through rope.
   C A huge lion who is awakened by a little mouse.
   D A little mouse who repays a lion's kindness.

The best answer to this question is "**D**." The story is about a lion who allows a mouse to go free, and is later saved by that mouse. The other choices are true, but they deal with only one part of the story.

Practice Exercises

> The laundry room in the back of my house is small and painted green. The door to the laundry room is made of frosted glass. This laundry room has always reminded me of Grandma. I saw her only once or twice a year because she lived in California.
>
> My favorite memory of Grandma was when she visited me in New York City. She took me to see a Broadway show. After the show, we waited for the subway train home. Somehow I got lost and was left on the subway platform. I remember yelling for grandmother and seeing her pink hat as she silently screamed to me behind the glass doors of that green subway car. I remember the train as it flew past me in a blur. When we were later reunited, I was so happy at being found. Grandma was so upset she was crying. That was the first time I felt connected to this woman I called Grandma.
>
> Now as I stand in the laundry room I remember her wrinkled face and white hair. I look at the frosted glass that I can never quite see through, just like the train's windows. And as I look around the laundry room, I am reminded of the woman who showed me her love that day.

1. **Which of these sentences best describes the passage?**
   A It is about a grandmother who grows old.
   B It is about a small, green laundry room.
   C It is about someone's memories of grandmother.
   D It is about how frightening it is to get lost.

CHECKING YOUR UNDERSTANDING

What is the answer to **Question 1**? _____ Explain your choice.

_____

CHAPTER 7

QUESTIONS ON VOCABULARY AND WORD ANALYSIS

After you have a general idea of what a reading is about, the next step is to make sure you understand any hard words in the reading. *Vocabulary questions* test your understanding of how a word or phrase is used in a passage. Such questions test how well you understand unfamiliar words or the use of words that have several meanings.

Some questions on the reading test will also examine your ability at word analysis. This chapter will help you practice with questions on both vocabulary and word analysis.

VOCABULARY QUESTIONS

Let's begin by looking at a sample vocabulary question. First, read the passage below. Then answer the question that follows.

> Jack was new in the neighborhood and decided to take a walk. During his stroll, Jack passed an old, dilapidated house on Mill Road. The windows of the house were broken, the roof appeared to leak, and no one had lived there for over twenty years.

1. **In this passage, "Jack passed an old, dilapidated house on Mill Road." What does *dilapidated* mean in this sentence?**
   A just built
   B very crowded
   C run down
   D made of stone

The best answer is "**D**." How can you answer such a question if you do not know the meaning of the word *dilapidated*? As you learned in Chapter 2, good readers use a variety of methods to figure out the meaning of strange words.

Let's review some of the techniques you can use when faced with answering questions about unfamiliar words or phrases:

★ **Examine surrounding words and sentences for context clues.** You can often find what something means by looking at the rest of the sentence and neighboring sentences. What is the author trying to say? What is the author's viewpoint?

★ **Figure out the part of speech of the unfamiliar word.** Is the unfamiliar word acting as a noun, verb, or some other part of speech? The correct answer will have to be the same part of speech.

★ **Use word analysis.** Break the word into *syllables* and try to pronounce the word. What does the word sound like? Check the word for familiar *prefixes, roots,* and *suffixes.* Break up *compound words* into parts.

★ **Substitute each answer choice for the word you are asked about.** Once you have looked at context clues and tried word analysis, turn to the choices. Read each choice in place of the word you are asked about. Focus on what you think the author is trying to say. Select the word or phrase that seems to make the most sense.

CHAPTER 7: QUESTIONS ON VOCABULARY AND WORD ANALYSIS   65

Let's practice answering a *vocabulary question*. Read the passage below. Then answer the question that follows.

> A powerful eagle seized a small lamb in her talons, and flew off with it to her nest. A nearby crow was watching and decided to copy the eagle. The crow swooped down and grabbed a large sheep. However, when the crow tried to fly away, it could not lift the sheep. Unlike the eagle, the crow's claws were not as strong.
>
> A nearby shepherd saw the crow and guessed what had happened. He caught the crow. That evening the shepherd gave the crow to his children. "What do you call it?" they asked. He replied, "This is a crow. But if you ask him, *he* would say he's an eagle."

2. In the phrase, "a powerful eagle seized a small lamb in her talons," what does the word *talons* mean?
   A Wings
   B Claws
   C Stomach
   D Eyes

CHECKING YOUR UNDERSTANDING

What is the answer to **Question 2**? _____ What clues helped you to figure out the meaning of the word *talons*? _____

_____

WORD ANALYSIS QUESTIONS

The ISAT test will have about 14 multiple-choice questions on word analysis. These questions will test your knowledge of *word sounds, prefixes, suffixes,* and *roots*. You have already learned about these in **Chapter 2.**

WORD SOUNDS

Questions on word sounds or phonics may show you the sound of a letter in a word and ask you to choose another word with the same sound.

3. **The boys entered the school *gym*. Which word begins with the same sound as *gym*?**

   A germ
   B good
   C great
   D gnat

   This question tests your knowledge of consonant sounds. "*G*" has two types of sounds: soft, like a "*j*," or hard, like the "*g*" in get. In the word *gym*, the "*g*" has a soft sound. In *germ*, the "*g*" has the same soft sound. In *good*, the sound of "*g*" is hard. In *great*, the word begins with a "*gr*" sound. In *gnat*, the "*g*" is silent. The correct answer is *germ*.

4. **When the car passed by, the boy *blinked*. What word begins with the same sounds as the word *blinked*?**

   A bin
   B black
   C book
   D bright

   This question also tests your knowledge of consonant sounds. The word *blinked* begins with the sounds "*b*" and "*l*." Both consonants are pronounced. Thus, the correct answer is *black* with the sound "*bl*."

5. **Which word has the same "*a*" sound as the letter "*a*" in *cake*?**
   A eat
   B weigh
   C hat
   D car

> This question tests your knowledge of vowel sounds. The "*a*" in *cake* is long — it says its name. The "*a*" in *eat* is silent. The "*a*" in *hat* is short. The "*a*" in *car* is changed by the "*r*." There is no letter "*a*" in *weigh*, but "*ei*" makes the long "*a*" sound in this word. The correct answer is *weigh*.

WORD PARTS

You already learned about *prefixes, suffixes, word roots,* and *compound words*. Some test questions will examine your knowledge of these word parts. Here is how some of these questions may appear:

6. **What does *discourage* mean?**
   A to give someone courage
   B to encourage
   C not to encourage
   D to have courage

> ***Discourage*** has two parts: the *root **courage*** and the *prefix **dis**.* **Dis** means *not*. To **dis•courage** is the opposite of encouraging someone. It means to take away a willingness to do something. The answer is *not to encourage*.

7. **What is the root of the word *bimonthly*?**
   A bi
   B month
   C monthly
   D ly

> The word **bimonthly** has a prefix **bi** and a suffix **ly**. The root of the word **bimonthly** is *month*. *Bimonthly* is an adverb which means something that is done twice a month: He was paid *bimonthly*.

Practice Exercises

Directions: Circle the best answer to the following questions.

1. What word has the same "e" sound as the letters "ea" in the word *eat*?
   - A feet
   - B fat
   - C get
   - D steak

2. Janet baked a *cake* for her sister's birthday. Which word BEGINS with the same sound as *cake*?
   - A circle
   - B cat
   - C clock
   - D sister

3. The student made a *graph*. Which word ENDS with the same sound as *graph*?
   - A laugh
   - B grab
   - C map
   - D show

4. The flashlight was *broken*. Which word BEGINS with the same sounds as *broken*?
   - A book
   - B blue
   - C rake
   - D brick

5. *Geography* is the study of the Earth's surface. *Geology* is the study of the rocks, minerals, and other materials that make up the Earth. What is a *geologist*?
   - A someone who studies the Earth's rocks and minerals
   - B someone who studies heat from the Earth
   - C someone who studies mathematics
   - D someone who makes maps

6. A *bilingual* person can speak two languages. A *bicycle* has two wheels. What is the meaning of the prefix *bi*?
   A one
   B two
   C three
   D many

7. What is the MEANING of the word *predetermined*?
   A determined before
   B not determined
   C to be determined later
   D to be determined again

8. What is the ROOT of the word *unhappiness*?
   A happy
   B un
   C happiness
   D ness

Use the following table to answer question 9.

Greek Word	Meaning
tele	far
scope	to see
phone	sound
micro	small

9. An instrument that allows us to see a long distance away is called a
   A telephone
   B telescope
   C microscope
   D microphone

Directions: Read the story and answer the *vocabulary and language questions* that follow.

BELLING THE CAT

The mice called a meeting to decide on *a course of action* to free themselves from their enemy, the cat. They wanted to find some way of knowing when the cat was coming to give them time to run away. The mice lived in such *trepidation* that they hardly dared stir from their dens by night or day.

Many plans were discussed at the meeting. However, none of them were thought to be good enough.

At last a young mouse in the room got up and said, "I have a plan that seems very simple, but I know it will be successful. All we need to do is to hang a bell around the cat's neck. When we hear the bell ringing, we'll know that the cat is coming."

All of the mice were surprised that they had not thought of such a simple plan before.

But *in the midst* of their rejoicing an old mouse arose and said. "I agree that the plan of the young mouse in the back of the room is very good. But let me ask one question during all of this celebrating and rejoicing: *"Which of us will put the bell on the cat?"*

Chapter 7: Questions on Vocabulary and Word Analysis 71

10. **The mice met to "decide on a course of action to free themselves from their enemy, the cat." What does *a course of action* mean?**
    A A plan to do something
    B How to join forces with a cat
    C A way to punish a cat
    D How to get more food

    What is the answer to **Question 10**? _____ Which clues helped you to figure out the meaning of the phrase? _____

    _____

11. **"The mice lived in such *trepidation* that they hardly dared stir from their dens by night or day." What does the word *trepidation* mean?**
    A Bravery
    B Fear
    C Debt
    D Pain

    What is the answer to **Question 11**? _____ Which clues helped you to figure out the meaning of the phrase? _____

    _____

12. **"In the midst of their rejoicing, an old mouse arose." What does the phrase *in the midst* mean?**
    A At the start
    B In the middle
    C At the end
    D A foggy moment

    What is the answer to **Question 12**? _____ Which clues helped you to figure out the meaning of the phrase? _____

    _____

CHAPTER 8

QUESTIONS ABOUT DETAILS IN A READING

In this chapter, you will learn how to answer questions that test your understanding of particular details in a reading. *Detail questions* focus on the **who, what, when, where,** and **how** by asking about particular facts in the reading. Sometimes a question may ask you which fact or detail shows that something takes place in the reading.

Detail questions about a **literary text** usually ask for details about the *setting, characters,* and *plot.* Here are some ways a *detail question* may appear on the test:

★ What is a character like?

★ What does a character do?

★ When does the story take place?

★ What shows that a character's feelings have changed?

★ How does a character feel about something?

Detail questions about an **informational text** usually ask about important supporting details and facts. Here is how some of these questions may appear:

★ What happened at a particular event?

★ When did events in the reading occur?

★ Where did the events in the reading take place?

★ Which facts support the author's viewpoint?

★ What does a person in the reading think or feel?

★ What shows that something has happened?

SCANNING TO FIND ANSWERS

For both literary and informational texts, the answer to a *detail question* will often be found directly in the reading. If you do not immediately recall the answer to the question, you should scan the reading. To **scan** is to look quickly through the text for specific information.

One way to scan is to look for *key words*. For example, if a question asks about a character's job in the story:

★ Look for where the character's name is mentioned.

★ Force your eyes to race along the page, but stop each time you see the name of the character.

★ Each time you stop, check the sentence to see if it mentions the character's job. If it does not, continue scanning the reading.

You may recall that in **Chapter 6** you learned about *skimming*. Although both *skimming* and *scanning* require you to read through a passage quickly, there are important differences between the two.

How Skimming and Scanning Differ

★ **Skimming.** When you skim, you read through a passage quickly *to get a general idea* of what the reading is all about. Use the title, subheadings, and captions under pictures as clues.

★ **Scanning.** When you scan, you read through a passage quickly *to locate specific information.* Once you locate the information you are looking for, read that sentence or section more slowly and carefully.

Sometimes the answer to a *detail question* will not be found directly in the passage. Instead you have to figure out the answer by using information from two or more places in the passage. You will learn more about using your thinking skills to answer such questions in a later chapter.

Let's practice answering *detail questions*. Read the passage on the next page. Then answer the questions that follow. The passage is adapted from the first chapter of a novel, *Half Magic,* by Edward Eager. The sentences have been numbered to help you find the answers quickly.

HOW IT BEGAN

1 It began one day in summer about thirty years ago, and it happened to four children.

2 Jane was the oldest and Mark was the only boy, and between them they ran everything.

3 Katherine was the middle girl, of a mild disposition and a comfort to her mother.

4 She knew she was a comfort, and easy-going, because she'd heard her mother say so.

5 And the others knew she was, too, by now, because ever since that day Katherine would keep boasting about what a comfort and how easy-going she was.

6 Finally, Jane declared she would utter a piercing shriek and fall over dead if she heard another word about it.

7 Martha was the youngest, and very difficult.

Now answer the following questions about the passage.

1. What time of year does this story begin?
  A Winter   C Spring
  B Fall   D Summer

> If you do not recall the answer to this question immediately, *scan* the passage. Look for some mention of one of the four seasons of the year.

CHECKING YOUR UNDERSTANDING

What is the answer to **Question 1**? _____ The first sentence states, "It began one day in *summer* about thirty years ago, and it happened to four children." Therefore, the answer is "**D**" — the story begins in summer.

2. **Who was the youngest child?**
   - A Jane
   - B Mark
   - C Martha
   - D Katherine

CHECKING YOUR UNDERSTANDING

What is the answer to **Question 2**? _____ In which sentence did you find the answer? _____

_____

3. **Which is the best description of Katherine?**
   - A She had a mild disposition.
   - B She never boasted.
   - C She made piercing shrieks.
   - D She was very difficult.

CHECKING YOUR UNDERSTANDING

What is the answer to **Question 3**? _____ In which sentence did you find the answer? _____

_____

4. **What shows that Katherine was a comfort to her mother?**
   A She felt she was very helpful.
   B She heard her mother say so.
   C Her little sister told her.
   D Her father told her.

> ### CHECKING YOUR UNDERSTANDING
>
> What is the answer to **Question 4**? _____ In which sentence did you find the answer? _____

5. **How did Jane feel about Katherine's repeating that she was a comfort to her mother?**
   A It made Jane happy to hear it.
   B Jane did not like Katherine's boasting.
   C It gave Jane a mild disposition.
   D Jane began to boast that she and Mark ran everything.

> ### CHECKING YOUR UNDERSTANDING
>
> What is the answer to **Question 5**? _____ To answer this question, you need to apply your reasoning powers to information in the story. The passage does not directly tell you how Jane felt about Katherine's boasting. It does tell you that Jane said she would utter a "piercing shriek" if Katherine boasted another time. From this reaction we can figure out that Jane disliked Katherine's boasting.

FACT AND OPINION QUESTIONS

Do you know the difference between a *fact* and an *opinion*? Some detail questions may ask you to identify a fact or an opinion.

FACT

A **fact** is a statement that can be shown to be correct or true. "The table is red" is a statement of fact. People can look at the table to see if it is red. Other facts can be checked by using other sources. Assume someone tells you that there was a fire yesterday at 42 Maple Lane. You can look in the newspaper, call the fire department, or even visit Maple Lane to check if there really was a fire.

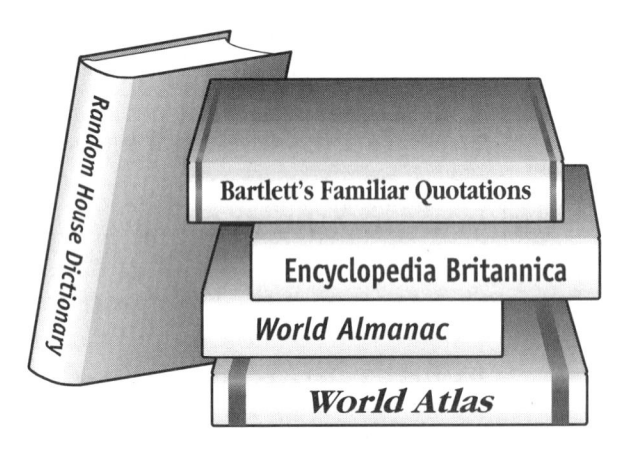

OPINION

An **opinion** is a statement of personal feelings or beliefs. Words such as *think, feel, probably,* and *believe* often show that a statement is an opinion. This statement is an opinion: "I believe George Washington was our greatest President." No one can prove Washington was our greatest President. The statement just tells us the writer's personal belief.

Sometimes writers make statements that look like facts but are actually opinions. Ask yourself: is this a fact that can be checked or is it an expression of the writer's feelings or beliefs?

Let's practice answering a *fact and opinion question*. Read the passage from "The Wandering Continent." Then answer the question.

Alfred Wegener was a curious man. He looked at the sky and wondered about the weather. He looked at the ocean and wondered what was under it. And when he looked at a map of the Earth, he wondered if it had always been the same. One day in 1911, Wegener came upon some books that showed the locations of fossils found around the world. Until then no one had proven why fossils of certain animals, like dinosaurs and snails, are found on lands so far apart. The animals were unable to swim across the ocean. Some scientists wondered if land "bridges" once connected the lands. Others thought that, if the continents were once part of a giant land mass, animals could have walked across before the land split up. Wegener became convinced that this was what had happened.

6. **Which of the following expresses an opinion about Wegener?**
   A He was a curious man.
   B He read some books showing fossil locations in 1911.
   C Fossils of the same animals have been found on lands that are far apart.
   D He believed separate areas were once part of a giant land mass.

CHECKING YOUR UNDERSTANDING

What is the answer to **Question 6**? _____ Explain your choice.

Practice Exercises

Directions: This article tells about life in ancient Egypt. Read the article. Then answer the questions that follow.

PASS THE BREAD, PLEASE
by Cyndy Hall

What did children eat in ancient Egypt? Did their parents make them finish their vegetables before dessert? Did kids have peanut butter and jelly sandwiches 4,000 years ago?

No one knows for sure if kids in ancient Egypt had to eat all their vegetables. But there are clues in the ruins of tombs that answer a lot of questions.

Families in ancient Egypt grew their own food. They planted beans, onions, cucumbers, and other crops. Farmers often took heads of "sacred lettuce" to temples to thank the gods for a good harvest. Fruit trees were everywhere. Children picked dates and figs for snacks.

The world's first beekeepers were Egyptians. Hives were kept in large pottery jars. Beekeepers simply brushed the bees aside to collect their honeycombs. The honey was stored in containers. Children must have enjoyed dipping their fingers in these bowls for a sweet treat.

Perhaps they put honey on their bread, too. Children ate bread at every meal. Bread was ancient Egypt's main food. There were hundreds of kinds of breads, in different shapes and sizes. Some recipes used fruits, garlic, or nuts to flavor the loaves.

CONTINUED

Eating bread caused some problems. Bits of desert sand and stones often got into the dough. Archaeologists have discovered that most Egyptian mummies have worn and missing teeth. They believe the Egyptians wore their teeth down while chewing on their bread.

So what did Egyptian children eat instead of peanut butter and jelly sandwiches? It's a recipe you'll probably not want to try at home. Children cut thick slabs of bread, spread garlic on top, and then piled on raw onions. Yummy? Maybe that's why they chewed mint leaves to sweeten their breath!

1. **What vegetable did ancient Egyptians take to their temples to thank their gods for a good harvest?**
   A Cucumbers
   B Beans
   C Lettuce
   D Onions

2. **What was the main food of most ancient Egyptians?**
   A Honey
   B Beans
   C Fruits
   D Bread

3. **Which shows that Egyptians had some problems eating bread?**
   A Mummies had worn teeth.
   B Children used garlic.
   C Lettuce was left in temples.
   D Children ate dates and figs.

4. **What did ancient Egyptian children eat instead of peanut butter and jelly sandwiches?**
   A Garlic and onion sandwiches
   B Bread and honey sandwiches
   C Mint leaf sandwiches
   D Bean and onion sandwiches

CHAPTER 9

QUESTIONS ABOUT CONNECTING DETAILS

Once you master the individual details of a reading, you can begin to make connections between these details. Connecting story details allows you to follow a series of events, explain why things happen, make comparisons, and draw conclusions from the reading.

Some multiple-choice questions on the **Grade 3 ISAT Reading Test** will examine your ability to draw connections among details. To make these connections, you have to apply your reasoning powers and background knowledge to what you read.

This chapter examines five types of questions that focus on connecting the details in a reading. You will notice that these test the strategies of good readers.

The types of questions that connect details are:

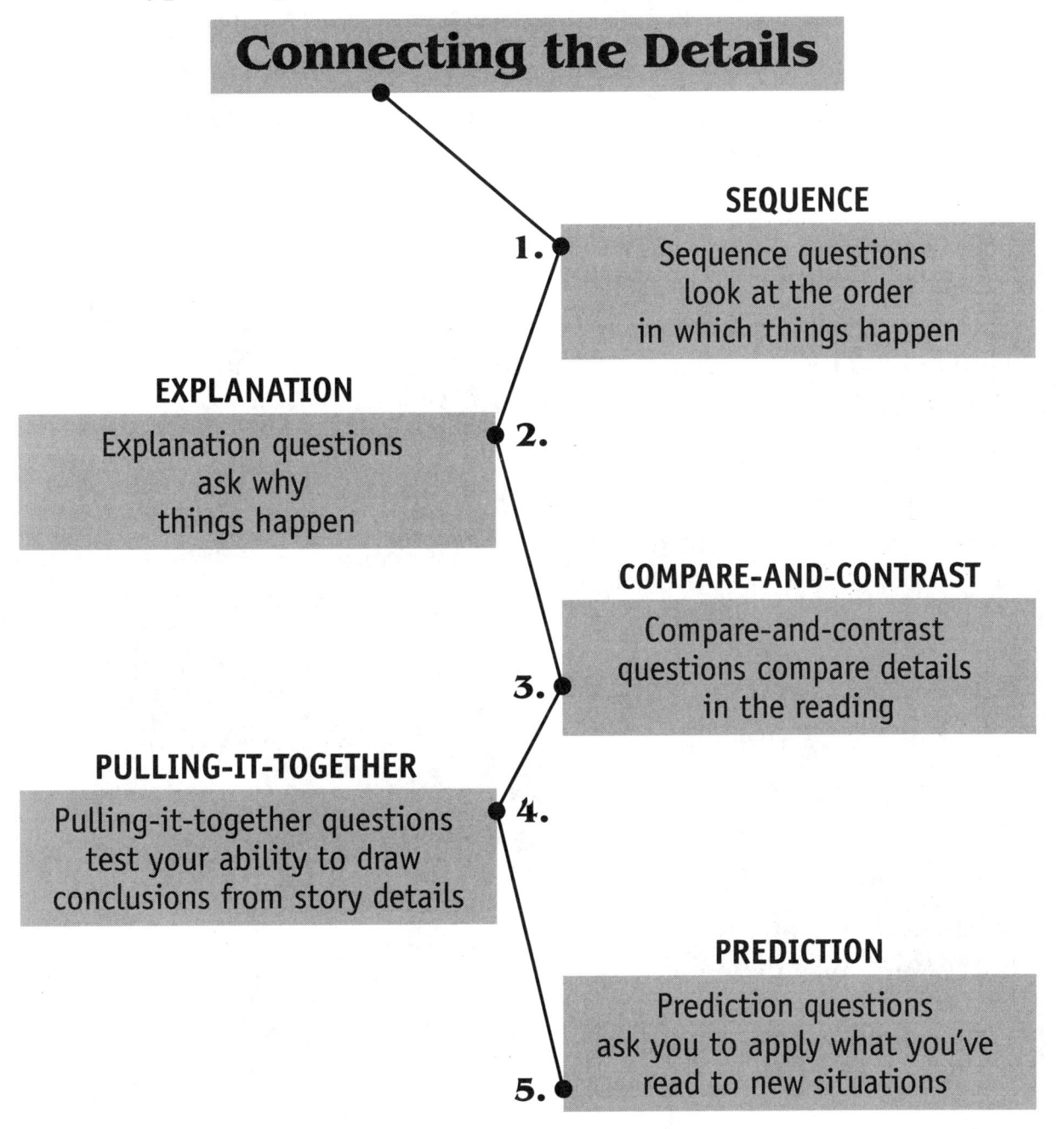

Connecting the Details

1. **SEQUENCE**
Sequence questions look at the order in which things happen

2. **EXPLANATION**
Explanation questions ask why things happen

3. **COMPARE-AND-CONTRAST**
Compare-and-contrast questions compare details in the reading

4. **PULLING-IT-TOGETHER**
Pulling-it-together questions test your ability to draw conclusions from story details

5. **PREDICTION**
Prediction questions ask you to apply what you've read to new situations

SEQUENCE QUESTIONS

Sequence questions test your ability to follow the order of events in a literary or informational reading. The answer can usually be found directly in the reading.

A writer will usually present events in the order in which they happened. Look for clue words to help you decide the sequence of events. These clue words include: **after, before, then, since, next, last,** and **first.** Look for hints about a change of time or season that may take place in the story.

Let's practice answering a *sequence question*. Read the passage below. Then answer the questions that follow.

> There once lived a farmer who owned the most wonderful goose. Every day, the goose laid a beautiful golden egg for him. The farmer sold each egg at the market. Soon he became very rich. But the farmer was impatient with the goose. It was giving him only one egg a day. He felt he was not getting rich fast enough.
>
> One day, he came up with an idea to get all the golden eggs at once. He decided he would cut the goose open and take out all the eggs. The farmer killed the poor goose. But when he opened it up, not a single golden egg was inside.
>
> And now his precious goose lay dead.

1. **Which event in the story occurred first?**
   A The farmer killed the goose.
   B The goose laid a golden egg each day.
   C The farmer decided to cut the goose open.
   D The farmer became very rich.

CHECKING YOUR UNDERSTANDING

What is the answer to **Question 1**? _____ What is the correct sequence of events in the story? _____
_____

2. **Which event happened last?**
   A The farmer sold an egg each day at the market.
   B The farmer became impatient with the goose.
   C The farmer opened up the goose but found no eggs.
   D The farmer decided to kill the goose.

CHECKING YOUR UNDERSTANDING

What is the answer to **Question 2**? _____ Explain your choice.
_____
_____

EXPLANATION QUESTIONS

When we read about events, we often think about *why* these things happened. An *explanation question* tests your understanding of cause-and-effect relationships.

★ The **cause** of something is what made it happen. For example, if you turn the switch of a light, you make it go on. The cause of the light's going on is your turn of the switch. Questions asking for the cause of something often begin with the question word *why.*

★ The **effect** of something is what happens as a result. The effect of your turning on the light switch is that the light goes on.

CAUSE
Someone turned on the switch.

EFFECT
The light went on.

Sometimes an event will have many causes and several effects. You can use a topic or sequence map to show *causes* and their *effects*. Use arrows to indicate cause-and-effect relationships. For example,

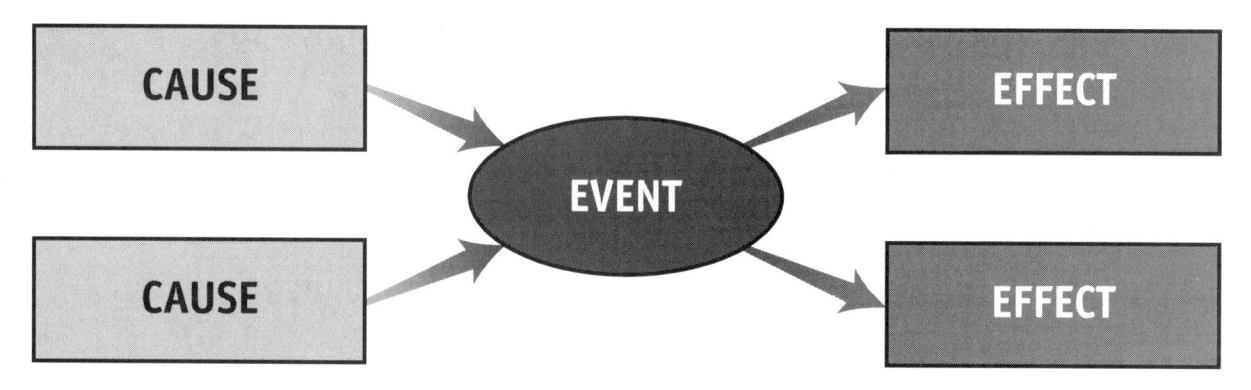

CAUSE → **EVENT** → **EFFECT**
CAUSE → **EVENT** → **EFFECT**

You should look for the answers to *explanation questions* in the reading itself. Often, clue words will alert you. Key words include: **why, because, as a result,** and **due to.** Sometimes you will not find these words in the reading, but it will still be clear that one event in the reading caused another. If the question asks **why** something happened, look through the passage to see the reasons why it occurred.

Quite often you will find that something happens in a story or in real life because of the actions of a character or a real-life person. Think about why the character acted as he or she did. What was the character trying to do? The **reason why** a character or person did something may help to explain why it happened. Always remember to think about the motives of the characters when answering an *explanation question*.

Let's practice answering an *explanation question*. Read the following passage. Then answer the questions that follow.

> An African chief had three sons. Each was talented in fighting and riding. Each son competed with his brothers to be the best. One day the chief decided to settle their constant arguing. He announced he would test his sons to see who had the greatest skills.
>
> The chief pointed to a tree next to their home. "I'll use this tree to test which of you is most talented," said the chief. The sons quickly mounted their horses. They rode off a distance and stopped.
>
> The eldest son raced his horse toward the tree. He thrust his spear through the tree and rode through the hole he had made. The second son raced his horse forward. When he reached the tree, he and his horse leaped over it.
>
> The youngest son went last. He rode forward, grabbed the tree and pulled it out, roots and all. He rode on, waving the tree over his head. Thrilled by this deed, the chief considered his youngest son to be the greatest one.

3. Why did the chief decide to hold a contest among his sons?
   A To see which son he loved the most
   B To see if his sons were truly loyal to him
   C To see who had the greatest skills
   D To see who would become the next chief

CHECKING YOUR UNDERSTANDING

What is the answer to **Question 3**? _____ Explain your choice.

_____

_____

4. **Why did the youngest son pull the tree out of the ground?**
   A He wanted to show he was more clever than his brothers.
   B He wanted to show how much he loved his mother.
   C He wanted to show he was angry with his father.
   D He wanted to show his strength and skill.

CHECKING YOUR UNDERSTANDING

What is the answer to **Question 4**? _____ Explain your choice.

_____

_____

_____

COMPARE-AND-CONTRAST QUESTIONS

Sometimes we compare things to understand them better. We want to know how they are different and how they are similar. A multiple-choice question may ask you to compare two *characters*, two *places*, or two *events*. You have to figure out how they are alike and how they are different. You may even be asked to compare the same character at different moments in the story.

The answer to a *compare-and-contrast question* is often found directly in the reading. Scan the passage until you find the things you must compare. Make a mental note about the features of each item. Then think about how the two items are similar and how they are different.

In **Chapter 3,** you learned to compare two items by using a Venn diagram. If time permits, it may help to write down the main similarities and differences in the form of a Venn diagram. Then you can answer the question more easily.

Let's practice answering a *compare-and-contrast question*. Read the following passage. Then answer the questions that follow.

Darrell and José were schoolmates. They were traveling together through the forest when suddenly a huge bear jumped out of the brush. Darrell, thinking of his own safety, climbed up a tree. José threw himself on the ground. He lay still, as if he were dead. José knew that bears will not touch a dead body. The bear sniffed at José's head awhile and then walked away. After the bear left, Darrell climbed down from the tree. He said, "It looked to me as if that bear whispered in your ear. What did he say?"

José answered coldly, "He said it's unwise to have a friend who runs away when you most need him."

5. **In what way were Darrell and José ALIKE?**
   A They enjoyed fighting bears.
   B They liked climbing trees.
   C They went to the same school.
   D They always helped each other.

> **CHECKING YOUR UNDERSTANDING**
>
> What is the answer to **Question 5**? _____ Explain your choice.
> _____
> _____
> _____

6. **How did José's feelings about Darrell change after they met the bear?**
   A José became less trusting of Darrell.
   B José grew jealous of Darrell.
   C José refused to talk to Darrell ever again.
   D José grew closer to Darrell as a friend.

> **CHECKING YOUR UNDERSTANDING**
>
> What is the answer to **Question 6**? _____ Explain your choice.
> _____
> _____
> _____

PULLING-IT-TOGETHER QUESTIONS

Pulling-it-together questions test your ability to draw conclusions from details in the reading. They call for you to apply your own reasoning powers. To answer a *pulling-it-together question,* use details in the reading as clues. Then apply your own thinking skills to identify the best answer.

For example, a *pulling-it-together question* might ask you to select a conclusion based on a series of facts in an informational reading:

> In the early 1800s, American pioneers settled the area around the Great Lakes. In order to survive, these pioneers had to cut down trees, plant fields with crops, and build their homes. A typical pioneer family worked from early morning until nightfall. Men would clear the land and plant the fields. At the same time, women helped with the farm animals, cooked, made clothes, and cared for the children.

7. **What conclusion can be made about the lifestyles of American pioneers in the early 1800s?**
   A Most pioneers came from the Northeast.
   B The pioneers were concerned about protecting nature.
   C Pioneer women worked just as hard as men.
   D The pioneers did not have any farm animals.

The answer is "**C.**" Although the passage does not compare the work of pioneer men and women, it lists the jobs each filled. It also explains that pioneers had to work from early morning until nightfall. From this, you can *draw the conclusion* that pioneer women worked just as hard as men.

Let's practice answering a *pulling-it-together question.* Read the following passage.

> Jerusalem is an ancient city in the Middle East. Today, it is located in the country of Israel. Palestinians, a group of Arabs in Israel, want to have their own country. They want Jerusalem to become their capital. Israeli Jews and Palestinian Arabs both consider Jerusalem to be a very holy city.

8. **What conclusion can be drawn from this passage?**
   A Most Israelis and Palestinians are friends.
   B Israelis and Palestinians disagree about the future of Jerusalem.
   C Jerusalem should continue to remain in Israel.
   D Jerusalem should become the capital of Palestine.

CHECKING YOUR UNDERSTANDING

What is the answer to **Question 8**? _____ Explain your choice.

PREDICTION QUESTIONS

After you have completed a reading, you should connect what you have learned with what you already know. *Prediction questions* test your ability to apply what you have learned from the reading to new situations. *Prediction questions* might appear as follows:

★ If the story could continue, what might happen next?

★ What might a character in the story do in a different situation?

To answer a *prediction question,* apply what you have learned in the story to the new situation. For example, you may read a story about a woman who was generous with her money. A *prediction question* might ask what would happen if she met a starving stranger. We could predict that the woman would try to help the person in need.

Let's practice answering a *prediction question*. Read the passage below. Then answer the question that follows.

> By 1871, about 300,000 people lived in Chicago. Most lived and worked in buildings made of wood. Sidewalks and many streets were made of wooden blocks. The summer and fall of 1871 were extremely dry. It hardly rained for months. Dry wooden buildings, lumberyards and grain storehouses were ready to ignite. On Sunday night, October 8th, a fire started in Mrs. O'Leary's barn in the city's center. Other wooden buildings quickly caught fire. The pumping house also burned, leaving Chicago's fire departments without water. The city burned for two days. About 300 Chicagoans died. More than 18,000 buildings were destroyed, and nearly 100,000 people were left homeless.

9. Based on the reading, what action would you predict Chicagoans to have taken following the Great Fire of 1871?
   A People rebuilt Chicago using mostly wood.
   B New laws required buildings to be made of fireproof materials.
   C Chicago closed down its fire department.
   D Most people moved out of Chicago.

CHECKING YOUR UNDERSTANDING

What is the answer to **Question 8**? _____ Explain your choice.

_____

Practice Exercises

Directions: Read the story below. Answer the questions that follow.

DAMON AND PYTHIAS

Damon and Pythias had been best friends since childhood. They trusted each other like brothers, each knowing the other would do anything for his friend.

The King of Syracuse grew annoyed when he heard about a speech Pythias was giving. Pythias was telling people that no man should have unlimited power. In a rage, the king summoned Pythias and his friend Damon. "Who do you think you are, spreading trouble among the people?" the king demanded.

"I spread only the truth," Pythias answered. "There can be nothing wrong with that."

CONTINUED

"And do you say that the king's laws are not good? This talk is treason," the king shouted. "Take back what you said or you'll face trouble." Pythias refused to take back anything he had said.

"Then you'll die," said the king. "Do you have any last requests?" Pythias asked the king to let him go home to put his house in order. The king laughed. "Do you think I'm stupid? If I let you leave the city, you will never return." Pythias said he would give the king a pledge.

"What pledge could you possibly give to make me think you'll ever return?" the king demanded.

At that instant Damon stepped forward. "I will be his pledge," he said. "Keep me here as your prisoner, until he returns. For sure Pythias will return so long as you hold me."

The king said, "Very well, but if you're willing to take your friend's place, you must also accept his punishment. If Pythias doesn't return, you'll die in his place." Damon replied that he had no doubt that Pythias would keep his word.

Pythias was set free, while Damon was put in prison. After several days, the king visited Damon to see if he was sorry he had made the bargain. "Time is almost up," the king said. "You're a fool to rely on a friend's promise. Did you think he would sacrifice his life for yours?"

CONTINUED

"He has been delayed," Damon answered. "He'll be here on time. I am as confident of this as I am of my own existence." The king was startled at his confidence, and left Damon in his cell.

The fatal day arrived. Damon was led before the executioner. The king greeted him with a smile. "It seems your friend failed to turn up," he laughed. "What do you think of him now?"

"He is my friend," Damon answered. "I trust him."

Just as he said this, Pythias staggered in, bruised and battered from exhaustion. He rushed to his friend. "You are safe," he gasped.

"My ship was wrecked in a storm, and then bandits attacked me on the road. But I refused to give up. I have come back to receive my punishment." The king heard his words with amazement. It was impossible to resist the power of such friendship.

"The sentence is cancelled," he declared. "I never believed such loyalty could exist in a friendship. You've shown me I was wrong. You shall be rewarded with your freedom. I ask only one favor."

"What is that?" the two friends asked.

The king answered, "Teach me how to be such a loyal friend."

1. **Which event in the story happened first?**
   A In a rage, the king summoned Damon and Pythias.
   B Pythias returned to save his friend.
   C Pythias asked the king to let him go home.
   D The king visited Damon in prison.

   `Sequence`

2. **What happened after Damon said he would take the place of his friend Pythias?**
   A The king agreed to let Pythias go home.
   B The king immediately set Pythias free.
   C The king had Damon arrested for speaking out.
   D The king refused to let Pythias leave for home.

   `Sequence`

3. **Why did the King of Syracuse have Pythias arrested?**
   A He was a ruler who arrested people for no reason.
   B He was jealous of the relationship between Pythias and Damon.
   C He was angry at a speech Pythias had given.
   D He feared a plot to overthrow him.

   `Explanation`

4. **What caused Damon to volunteer as a stand-in for Pythias?**
   A Pythias owed Damon a favor.
   B They were very good friends.
   C Damon wanted Pythias to continue making speeches.
   D Damon knew the king was afraid to execute Pythias.

   `Explanation`

5. **Why didn't Pythias return until the last moment?**
   A He could not make up his mind whether or not to return.
   B His return was delayed by events beyond his control.
   C He was afraid to be executed.
   D His friendship with Damon was over.

   `Explanation`

6. **What effect did the return of Pythias have on the king?**
   A The king ruled that Damon and Pythias could no longer be friends.
   B The king had both men arrested.
   C The king wanted to learn how to become a loyal friend.
   D The king was angered when he found that Pythias had returned.

   Explanation

7. **What was one way in which Damon and Pythias were ALIKE?**
   A They both spoke out against the king.
   B They were the same age.
   C They were willing to betray each other if necessary.
   D They were willing to sacrifice their lives for each other.

   Compare-and-Contrast

8. **Which term best describes the character of Pythias?**
   A Loyal   C Incapable
   B Foolish   D Cowardly

   Pulling-It-Together

9. **If Pythias had failed to return, how might this story have ended?**
   A The king would have set Damon free.
   B Damon would have tried to escape from prison.
   C The king would have executed Damon.
   D The king would have become good friends with Pythias.

   Prediction

10. **If Damon had been arrested instead of Pythias, how would Pythias have behaved?**
    A He also would have volunteered to take his friend's place.
    B He would have turned against Damon.
    C He would have fled the city.
    D He would have helped the king imprison Damon.

    Prediction

CHAPTER 10

QUESTIONS ON THE MAIN IDEA OR THEME

In **Chapter 6,** you learned about questions that test your opening or general impression of a reading. In later chapters, you learned about questions that test your understanding of details in the reading. After you have carefully read all the details, you should mentally step back from the reading passage and think to yourself:

> **What was the message or main idea of this reading?**

The details in the reading passage should help you to do more than just tell what the reading is mostly about. They should help you to understand the author's *main idea* or *theme*.

You have already learned that every informational reading has a ***main idea.*** The main idea is the message that the author is trying to communicate. It is what the author has to say about the topic. The rest of the reading gives details that support or explain the main idea.

A person who writes a story or other literary text also usually has a message. However, in a story the message is not called a main idea. Instead, the message of the author is called the ***theme*** of the story. A story can have more than one message or theme. Each theme is a lesson that the story teaches.

FINDING THE MAIN IDEA OF AN INFORMATIONAL READING

Think of the main idea as a newspaper headline. In one short sentence or phrase, a headline summarizes what the entire story says.

Read the following paragraph. Then write a headline that expresses its main idea.

> Marco Polo was born in Venice in 1254. In those days most people did not travel far from their homes. Marco was only 17 years old when his father and uncle, two wealthy Italian merchants, decided to take him along on their travels.
>
> Marco traveled thousands of miles with them. They passed through the mountains and deserts of Turkey, Persia, and Afghanistan. The journey took more than three years. Marco was twenty years old when they finally reached the empire of China. Few Europeans had even heard of China at that time.
>
> *Marco Polo arrives in China*

Now, write a headline expressing the main idea of this reading. Remember, the main idea tells about the whole passage, not just specific details.

Someone who reads your headline should have a good idea of what the passage says:

_____

_____

A multiple-choice question on the **Grade 3 ISAT Reading Test** may ask you about the main idea. Such questions might appear as:

★ What is the *main idea* of the passage?

★ Which sentence **best summarizes** what the author is saying?

All of these questions have *one thing* in common. They test your understanding of what you have read. They all ask you for the **main idea** of the passage.

To answer a *main idea question* about an informational reading, first think about the topic of the reading. Then think about the author's message about that topic. Sometimes the author may state the main idea in a single sentence. At other times, you will have to figure out the main idea. Think of a single sentence that sums up the passage and what the author is writing about.

Next, look at the answer choices. Select the answer that *best summarizes* what the whole reading is about. Choices that focus only on specific details in the reading rather than the whole passage are probably incorrect answers.

If you are not sure which answer is best, review the passage a second time by **skimming** — reading the passage quickly to get a sense of what the author is focusing on.

Let's practice a *main idea question*. Read the informational passage on the next page. Then answer the question that follows.

The temperature of the water in the Antarctic and Arctic Oceans is below freezing most of the year. The water surface is likely to be covered with ice for ten months of the year. Fish, such as the dragonfish, swim in the very cold waters below the ice. Salt in the water helps to keep this water from freezing. A special sugar-like substance in the blood of the fish, called glycopeptide, helps to keep ice from forming inside the fish. Like antifreeze in a car's radiator, it keeps the water from turning into ice. Glycopeptide keeps the blood of these fish from freezing. This natural antifreeze sticks to any tiny ice crystals that form in the blood. The glycopeptide prevents the crystals from growing large enough to be damaging.

1. What is the main idea of this passage?
   A Water in the Arctic and Antarctic Oceans is below freezing most of the year.
   B A sugar-like substance in the blood of some fish allows them to swim in freezing-cold saltwater.
   C Glycopeptide is the name of a substance found in the blood of the dragonfish.
   D Antifreeze keeps the water in a car radiator from turning to ice.

The correct answer to this question is "B." The article explains that some fish can swim in the salt water of the Arctic and Antarctic, even though it is below freezing temperatures. A sugar-like substance prevents their blood from freezing. The other choices, although *correct* statements, are *not* the right answer. They focus on details in the article, not on the article's main idea.

FINDING THE THEME OF A STORY

You already know that a story may have one or more themes. A **theme** is like the main idea of a reading. It is the most important message that the story tells. Details in the story develop the message. Themes provide lessons about life and human nature. For example, in *The Golden Touch,* we learn that it is wrong to be greedy. The story explains this theme by telling what happened to King Midas.

Some questions will ask about the theme of a story. Sometimes the theme is stated directly in the story. At other times, you need to figure out the theme. To find the theme, ask yourself the question in the box. Your answer will lead you to the theme of the story.

> What lesson about life did I learn from reading this story?

Let's practice answering a *theme question* about a story. First read the passage below.

"Why do you walk sideways?" said a mother crab to her young son. "You should walk straight with your toes turned out." Not sure what to do, the son said, "Show me how to walk, mother." The young crab was very respectful, and always did as his mother said. So the mother crab tried to walk forward. After several failed attempts, she could only walk sideways like her son. And every time she turned her toes out, she tripped and fell on the sand. The mother crab thought to herself that today she had learned an important lesson from her son.

Now think about and write your answer to the following question.

> ### BEING AN ACTIVE READER
>
> What lesson about life did I learn from reading this story?
> _____
> _____
> _____
> _____
> _____

Now answer this multiple-choice question.

2. **What lesson can we learn from this story?**
   A You should never expect thanks from those you help.
   B You are judged by the company you keep.
   C Don't tell others how to act unless you can do it yourself.
   D Take what you can get when you can get it.

The correct answer to this question is "**C.**" The mother crab tries to tell her son what to do, but she is unable to walk straight herself. The message of the story is that we should not order others to do things that are so hard that we cannot do them ourselves. The other choices are not lessons that are found in the story.

Practice Exercises

Directions: Read the story. Then answer the question that follows.

COME RAIN OR SHINE
by Geary Smith

Years ago, there lived an old woman with two sons. The old woman was very poor. She depended on her sons to take care of her with money they earned in their businesses.

The woman's older son sold fans. Her younger son sold umbrellas. Every day, she worried about their businesses, praying they would make a lot of money.

Every morning at sunrise, the woman looked up to the sky. When it was cloudy and dark, she'd say, "If the sun doesn't shine today, nobody will want to buy my son's fans, and he won't make any money."

When the sun was shining, she'd say, "I'm sure nobody will want to buy umbrellas from my son today, and he won't make any money."

No matter how the sky looked, sunny or cloudy, the woman worried.

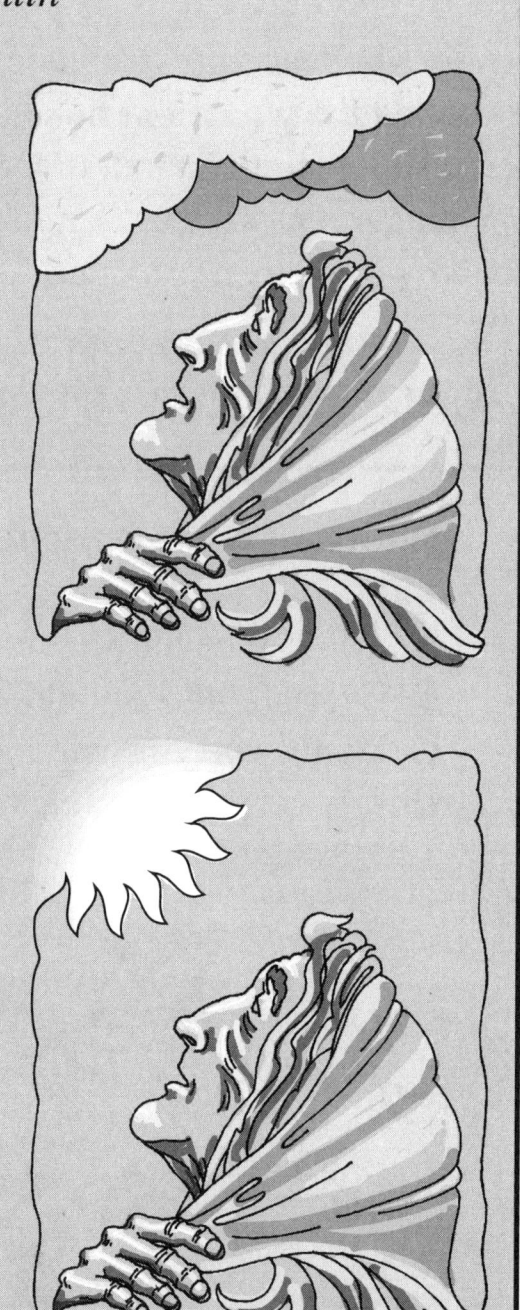

CONTINUED

One evening, while fretting about the sort of weather the next day might bring, she came upon a close friend who knew of her situation.

"Do you think it will be sunny or cloudy tomorrow?" the old woman asked her friend.

"My dear, you should never worry what tomorrow will bring," replied the woman's friend. "You have two hard-working sons. If the sun is shining, your older son will make money. If it rains, your younger son will make money. No matter what tomorrow brings, you will be well provided for."

The woman thought about what her friend told her, and she was happy and content for the rest of her days.

1. Which of these sentences best summarizes what this story shows?
   A You can never be sure about the weather.
   B Every mother should have two hard-working sons.
   C Don't worry if you don't really have a problem.
   D It is very frightening to grow old.

CHAPTER 11

ANSWERING EXTENDED-RESPONSE QUESTIONS

On the **Grade 3 ISAT Reading Test,** you will be asked to answer two extended-response questions. You will have one extended-response question on the second session and another on the third session of the test.

An **extended-response question** differs from a multiple-choice question. Unlike a multiple-choice question, an extended response question requires you to do more than select the best choice from four possible answers. Instead, you must write down your answer. You should write one or two paragraphs when answering each extended-response question.

STEPS IN ANSWERING THE QUESTION

There are three main steps in answering any extended-response question.

1. ANALYZE THE QUESTION
2. PLAN AND WRITE YOUR ANSWER
3. REVIEW AND REVISE

STEP 1: ANALYZE THE QUESTION

An extended-response question will give specific directions on what you should write. You will learn more about different types of extended-response questions later in this chapter. Be sure you understand the question before you move to the next step.

STEP 2: PLAN AND WRITE YOUR ANSWER

Take time to think about your answer. Review the passage to gain ideas and information. Jot down notes with details from the reading. Then turn your notes into a plan for writing your answer. Use an outline, topic map, or other format you prefer. Identify what you are writing about with an introduction. After you finish your plan, write your answer by turning each point into a complete sentence.

STEP 3: REVIEW AND REVISE YOUR ANSWER

When you have finished, read over answer. Make sure you answered the question. In addition, be sure that what you have written makes sense to you. Cross out any information that does not belong. Add any important ideas or details you may have left out.

TYPES OF EXTENDED-RESPONSE QUESTIONS

Extended-response questions focus on your understanding of the reading. You are expected to show that you understand the text, and also that you can *analyze* and *interpret* what you have read. Most extended-response questions ask you about the **what, why,** and **how** of a passage. These words provide the key to what you need to do.

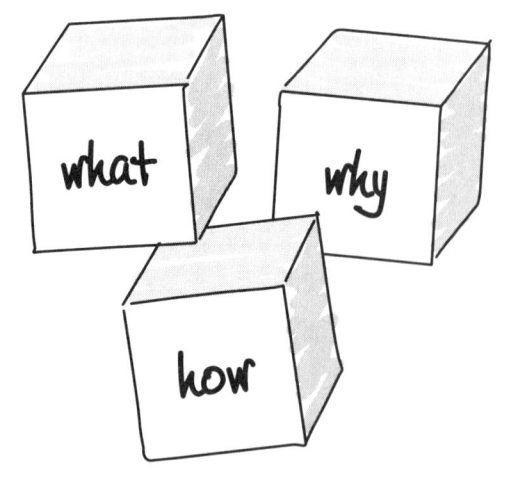

You already studied these question words in **Chapter 3.** Let's look at each of these question words again to see how they might appear in an extended-response question.

WHAT QUESTIONS

The question word *what* asks you to identify, explain, or describe specific things in a reading passage.

Here are examples of how you might see a *what question:*

> ★ *What* did King Midas do to help the friend of Dionysus?
>
> ★ *What* did Midas ask for when he was granted a wish?
>
> ★ *What* was the main lesson of the story?

To answer a *what question,* first think about what the question asks for. Do you have to identify something, explain it, or describe it? Look over the reading to get ideas for answering the question. Next, jot down your ideas using some type of note form or graphic organizer.

Now you are ready to answer the question. Begin with a **topic sentence** that tells your reader what you are trying to *identify, explain,* or *describe.* The simplest way to form the topic sentence is to echo the question. **Echoing the question** means you repeat part of the question as a statement. Then use details from the reading as supporting details for the rest of your paragraph.

Let's look at a model answer to the last question above.

> *What* was the main lesson of the story?
> Explain your answer using details from the story.

> [This topic sentence echoes the question and gives the story's main lesson.]

The main lesson of the story is that what we wish for often is not what is best for us. King Midas wanted the golden touch. He soon realized that this wish was really a curse. Midas could have all the gold he wanted, but he could not enjoy eating a piece of bread or drinking a glass of water. In the end, Midas realized that the simple pleasures in life, like eating and drinking, are more important than having gold. What he had thought he wanted was not really the best thing for him.

[This sentence uses details and examples directly from the story to support the topic sentence.]

[The final sentence provides a strong conclusion to the paragraph by summing up the main idea.]

CHECKING YOUR UNDERSTANDING

Now you try it.

What did King Midas do to earn a wish from Dionysus? Explain your answer using details from the story.

_____

_____

_____

_____

HOW QUESTIONS

How means "in what way." **How questions** look at what things are like in a reading, the way something happens in a reading, or the way something changes. Here are some examples of **how questions:**

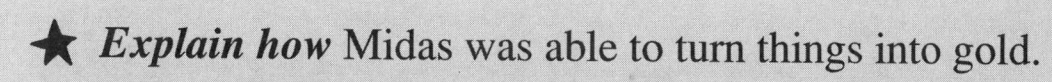

> ★ *Explain how* Midas was able to turn things into gold.
>
> ★ *Tell how* Midas changed after he received the golden touch.

Let's look at a model answer to the last question above.

> *Tell how* Midas changed
> after he received the golden touch.
> Explain your answer using details from the story.

[This topic sentence echoes the question.]

[This part tells what Midas was like before he received the golden touch.]

King Midas changed after he received the golden touch. Before he had the golden touch, all he thought about was getting rich. When he first received the golden touch, everything he touched turned to gold. Midas soon found that anything he tried to eat or drink also turned to gold. He became hungry and thirsty. Midas went to Dionysus and begged him to take away the golden touch. Midas learned that simple pleasures in life are more important than having gold.

[This shows how Midas changed after he received the golden touch.]

CHECKING YOUR UNDERSTANDING

Explain how the golden touch of King Midas turned out to be a curse. Explain your answer using details from the story.

_____

_____

_____

_____

WHY QUESTIONS

Why questions look at causes and effects. A **why question** may ask you to give one or more reasons **why** something happened. A **why question** might also ask you for the effects of an event. Here are some typical examples of the ways a **why question** might appear:

★ *Why did Dionysus grant King Midas one wish?*

★ *Explain why Midas became unhappy with the golden touch.*

When you answer a **why question,** first think about whether the question asks for *causes* or *effects*.

★ If the question asks about causes, think about the forces or events that caused the action or event to take place.

★ If the question asks why a character did something, think about the reasons that led the character to act that way.

★ If the question asks about effects, think about what happened because of that action or event.

CHAPTER 11: ANSWERING EXTENDED-RESPONSE QUESTIONS   113

Let's look at a model answer to the second question on the previous page.

> ***Explain why*** Midas became unhappy
> with the golden touch.
> Explain your answer using details from the story.

[This topic sentence echoes the question and states the main idea of the paragraph.]

[This part of the paragraph uses story details to explain why Midas became disappointed.]

King Midas became unhappy with the golden touch. The golden touch gave Midas the power to turn everything he touched to gold. Midas soon discovered he could not enjoy the simple pleasures of life, like eating and drinking. Whenever he tried to eat or drink something, it turned to gold. Because Midas quickly grew hungry and thirsty, he became unhappy with the golden touch. He realized the golden touch was really a curse, not a gift.

[The last two sentences concludes the paragraph by summing up why Midas was disappointed.]

CHECKING YOUR UNDERSTANDING

What effects did the golden touch have on King Midas? Explain your answer using details from the story.

_____
_____
_____

CHAPTER 12

TESTING YOUR UNDERSTANDING

This chapter will require you to read two passages. The first is an informational reading. The second is a literary text. Each passage is followed by a group of multiple-choice and extended-response questions. These questions test your understanding of different types of questions you have learned about in the last six chapters.

This practice test has two sessions. You should take about **40 minutes** to read each passage and complete the questions in that session. Try to time yourself. This will help you get an idea of how long it will take to complete the real **Grade 3 ISAT Reading Test.**

On this practice test, each question is identified by its type. These clues are included to help you focus on the type of question being asked. However, these clues will **NOT** be provided to you when you take the actual reading test.

START OF SESSION 1

Directions: First, you are going to read a passage with the title "The Celebrated Frogs with Missing Legs." Then you will answer several questions about what you have read. You may look back at the passage as often as you like. Now begin.

The Celebrated Frogs With Missing Legs
adapted from Susan Hayes

In the summer of 1999, eight students and their teacher were hiking in the woods near Henderson, Minnesota, as part of their study of the environment. But they soon came upon some frogs with twisted legs. "At first, we thought the frogs had broken their legs," said one of the students. "Then we found three or four frogs that were missing a leg."

The students headed to a nearby pond to search for more frogs. "The closer we got to the pond, the more problems we found," said another student. By the end of the day, they caught 22 frogs. Half of them had serious deformities.

The case of the frogs with missing legs alarmed scientists across the country. Scientists wanted to know what had happened to the frogs, and if what affected them could affect us.

The students wrote down their findings and returned to school with three of the frogs with missing legs. Because they found so many frogs with deformities, they thought the cause might be from chemicals sprayed on the surrounding farmland. They called the farmer who lived nearby to find out what pesticides he used. They placed queries on the Internet, asking if anyone else had seen similar frogs. Their teacher called the Minnesota Pollution Control Agency (*known as the M.P.C.A.*), a state agency that protects the environment.

CONTINUED

The M.P.C.A. decided to investigate. What happens to frogs is important because frogs act as early warning signs of a problem with the environment. Because their skin is so thin, they are easily hurt by poisons in both the air and water.

The M.P.C.A. immediately sent a researcher to the pond. The students were not content just to let the scientists take over. M.P.C.A. researchers assigned the students to find a control site — a place where there weren't any frogs with missing limbs.

"We must have checked out more than a dozen ponds," says Cindy. "We'd catch 100 normal frogs, but then we'd go back and find frogs with deformities."

News of the students' discovery spread. Reports started coming in from other states and foreign countries that similar outbreaks had been spotted. The frog mystery became an ongoing science project at the school. The kids — there were now 12 of them — were called the "Frog Group." Once a week, they headed for the pond, tested the water, and sent their results to the M.P.C.A.

Members of the group have testified before the state legislature to obtain funding for an educational program on frogs. They've created their own special frog web site. They even created an exhibit about the project at the Minnesota Zoo. They have appeared on television shows, including the Discovery Channel.

CONTINUED

> Today, scientists don't appear any closer to an explanation. The M.P.C.A. believes some kind of pollution in the water may be causing the deformities. Other scientists insist that the cause may be a natural one, such as parasites.*
>
> "We're not sure what's causing it," says a Frog Group member. "Maybe it's a combination of things. Our goal is to inform people as to what is going on." Whoever finally solves the mystery, the students can take credit for finding it.
>
> ---
>
> *__parasite__ – an animal or plant that lives off another animal or plant for its nutrients.

> Each question is identified by its type. If you get a particular question wrong, re-read the section that tells you how to answer this type of question.

1. **What is this article mostly about?**
   - A How young children learn
   - B The importance of frogs in our lives
   - C The mystery of the frogs with deformities
   - D The important role played by the M.P.C.A.

   [Opening Impressions]

2. **In the article, students "placed queries on the Internet, asking if anyone else had seen similar frogs." What are *queries*?**
   - A Questions
   - C Quotes
   - B Clever remarks
   - D Reports

   [Vocabulary]

3. Who first discovered that some frogs were missing legs?
   - A A school principal
   - B Students
   - C The M.P.C.A
   - D Scientists

   Specific Detail

4. When did the events in this article first begin?
   - A In the summer
   - B At the start of fall
   - C During winter
   - D At the end of spring

   Specific Detail

5. Where did the students find most of the frogs with deformities?
   - A In orchards on a farm
   - B In the woods near ponds
   - C In a city sewer system
   - D Under mobile homes

   Specific Detail

6. What is the main job of the M.P.C.A.?
   - A It helps students learn about the environment.
   - B It brings criminals to trial.
   - C It is responsible for protecting the environment.
   - D It provides scientific information over the Internet.

   Specific Detail

7. What shows that the M.P.C.A. became concerned by the students' discovery?
   - A Scientists across the country were concerned.
   - B The M.P.C.A. started an investigation.
   - C The students spoke to a nearby farmer about his pesticides.
   - D The students' teacher called the M.P.C.A.

   Specific Detail

8. **Which sentence from the article expresses an opinion?**
   - A The frogs without legs alarmed scientists.
   - B The students documented their findings and returned to school.
   - C The students helped the M.P.C.A. collect frogs with missing legs.
   - D Some kind of pollution in the water may be causing the deformities.

   Fact/Opinion

9. **Which of these events in the article occurred first?**
   - A The students asked the farmer about the pesticides he used.
   - B Eight students were hiking in the woods to study the environment.
   - C The students appeared on television.
   - D The students created an exhibit at the zoo.

   Sequence

10. **Why did the students become alarmed during their hike in the woods?**
    - A They discovered all the ponds in the state had been polluted.
    - B Most of the frogs they found were dead.
    - C They found a large number of frogs without legs.
    - D Scientists had warned them not to go into the woods.

    Explanation

11. **Which word best describes the students in this article?**
    - A curious
    - B immature
    - C affectionate
    - D uncaring

    Pulling-It-Together

12. **Which explains why the M.P.C.A. and scientists were alarmed about the frogs with missing legs?**
    - ○ A Frogs act as early warning signs of environmental problems.
    - ○ B Fishermen need frogs as bait to catch fish.
    - ○ C People who eat frogs may catch their diseases.
    - ○ D Frogs are an endangered species. [Explanation]

13. **What shows that there is no agreement on what is causing the frogs to have missing legs?**
    - ○ A Scientists are unsure if pollution or parasites caused the frogs to be missing legs.
    - ○ B The M.P.C.A. stopped investigating the frogs.
    - ○ C The students have formed the Frog Group.
    - ○ D A local farmer is still using pesticides. [Explanation]

14. **What event would solve the "mystery" in the article?**
    - ○ A The school would allow students to take a class studying the environment.
    - ○ B Scientists would find the reason why frogs were missing legs.
    - ○ C The students would become scientists when they reached adulthood.
    - ○ D The state legislature would vote that the mystery was solved. [Prediction]

15. **"Other scientists insist that the cause may be a natural one, such as parasites." What are *parasites*?**
    - ○ A Man-made chemicals
    - ○ B Creatures that live off others
    - ○ C A type of hurricane
    - ○ D An unusual warming of the Earth [Vocabulary]

EXTENDED-RESPONSE QUESTION

16. Why were the students so interested in the mystery of the frogs? Use details from the reading passage to support your answer.

_____
_____
_____
_____
_____
_____
_____
_____
_____

END OF SESSION 1

START OF SESSION 2

Directions: In this session, you will read a passage with the title, "The Recital." After you read the passage, answer the questions that follow. You will have **35 minutes** to complete this session. You may look back at the passage as often as you like. Now begin.

THE RECITAL
by Kathleen Benner Duble

"Hannah?" Mama said, bending down to her. "Are you all right?"

Hannah nodded yes. But it wasn't true. Since this morning her stomach had been doing flips like that day on the water slide when it kept going faster and faster and wouldn't slow down. When she had reached the bottom, she threw up on the sidewalk in front of millions of people. Thinking of this made Hannah feel even sicker.

"You're not nervous, are you?" Mama asked. Hannah shook her head no.

"Why would she be scared?" Mary piped up. "She only has to play 'Twinkle, Twinkle, Little Star.' It's so easy I never practice it anymore. Besides, I'll be playing it with her. I'm the one who should be scared."

At the mention of "Twinkle," Hannah felt her stomach turn again. She thought of the piano waiting at Mrs. Johnson's studio, and her mouth suddenly felt dry and sticky. Mary picked up her violin and began to play a piece of music. It sounded beautiful to Hannah. It was something that would be too hard for her to play.

"I should be very nervous," Mary said, "I have to play three pieces tonight. But I'm not scared."

Hannah knew Mary was not scared. Mary was never scared. Hannah wished she were more like Mary. Hannah stared at her own white blouse, dark skirt, white tights, and black shoes. She felt like a zebra.

CONTINUED

Papa came into the room and scooped up Mary. "So, it's the big night, is it? I can't wait to hear my little musicians play." He grinned at Hannah. Hannah forced herself to smile back.

Papa hugged her against him, still holding Mary. "To the car," he said, "and on to Mrs. Johnson's studio."

Backstage, Hannah's hands were cold and damp as she felt on edge. All around, students were tuning their instruments — accordions, trumpets, and clarinets. Hannah peeked through the closed curtains at the stage. It looked huge. The piano looked as if it could open its lid and eat her.

"Places, everyone!" called Mrs. Johnson. Mary danced into line behind Hannah and the other younger children.

"Aren't you supposed to be back here with us, Mary?" an older girl whispered.

"I have to play with my sister first," Mary whispered back. "Then I'll be back here." Mary put her hand in Hannah's hand and squeezed it tight. "It'll be all right," she said softly. Weakly, Hannah squeezed back.

The curtain opened. The recital began. One child played, then another. Soon, she heard Mrs. Johnson announce her name and Mary's name. Slowly Hannah walked on to the stage with Mary behind her. Hannah's legs felt weak. The lights were bright.

CONTINUED

Quickly, Hannah walked to the piano. Mary stood by her, and they bowed. There was clapping, and once again, Hannah felt an awful taste in her mouth. When the clapping stopped, Hannah slid onto the piano bench. Mary put her violin to her chin and smiled at Hannah.

Mary nodded, and Hannah began to play. She thought about playing and nothing else. Suddenly, Hannah heard something odd. Mary was not playing "Twinkle." Hannah didn't know what Mary was playing. Hannah couldn't believe it. Her sister, Mary, was making a mess out of a simple song like "Twinkle."

Hannah glanced over at Mary. Her face was white, and her hands were trembling on the violin. Then Hannah realized what had happened. Mary had forgotten the notes, and now she was scared.

"I should have practiced," Mary thought, almost crying. Hannah began whispering the notes to the song to Mary — *A, A, E, E, F-sharp* …. Slowly, Mary hit the notes in time with Hannah's playing. When they finished, they finished together.

The clapping was loud in Hannah's ears. When they bowed, Hannah took Mary's hand and squeezed. Mary's hand was damp and cold, but Hannah's hand was dry and warm. Backstage, Mary didn't say a word, but ran off to be with her friends.

"Were you nervous?" Hannah heard someone ask Mary. "Who, me?" said Mary. "I'm never scared."

Just then, Mary turned and caught Hannah's eye. Mary smiled, and Hannah smiled back. Hannah would never tell. Mary was her sister. Besides, deep inside Hannah, there was a place that felt comforted knowing that Mary, too, could be scared.

1. **What is the story mostly about?**
   - A Learning how to practice a musical instrument
   - B Hannah and Mary's relationship with their parents
   - C How two sisters act during a recital
   - D Playing a piano

   `Opening Impressions`

2. **In this story, Hannah and her sister Mary are at a recital. What does *recital* mean?**
   - A The tuning of musical instruments
   - B A musical performance
   - C Practicing a musical instrument
   - D A meeting with other children

   `Vocabulary`

3. **In the story, Hannah's hands were cold and damp as she felt "on edge." What does *on edge* mean?**
   - A Nervous
   - B Never-ending
   - C Neighborly
   - D Sickly

   `Vocabulary`

4. **What happened to Hannah on the day she went for a ride on the water slide?**
   - A She enjoyed herself tremendously.
   - B She fell down and sprained her ankle.
   - C She became ill and threw up.
   - D She played the piano for some strangers.

   `Specific Detail`

5. **What musical instrument did Mary play?**
   - A The piano
   - B A violin
   - C A trumpet
   - D An accordion

   `Specific Detail`

6. **In the story, what do *A, A, E, E, F-sharp* stand for?**
   - A The notes to a song in the story
   - B The words to "Twinkle, Twinkle, Little Star"
   - C A secret code used by Mary and Hannah
   - D The sound made by dance steps

   `Specific Detail`

7. **Which is a factual statement about Mary?**
   - A Mary should have practiced more.
   - B Mary was a better musician than Hannah.
   - C Mary never got scared.
   - D Mary was Hannah's older sister.

   [Fact/Opinion]

8. **Which shows that Mary was nervous?**
   - A She told Hannah that she was nervous.
   - B She felt an awful taste in her mouth.
   - C Her face turned white.
   - D She told her friends.

   [Specific Detail]

9. **What happened when Mary forgot the notes to "Twinkle"?**
   - A Hannah took Mary's hand and squeezed it.
   - B Hannah told everyone Mary forgot how to play the song.
   - C Hannah began whispering the notes to the song to Mary.
   - D Mary admitted her nervousness when she played the song.

   [Sequence]

10. **What led Hannah to become nervous in the story?**
    - A She was afraid of making her mother angry.
    - B She feared playing at the recital.
    - C She was worried she would offend Mary.
    - D She feared her father.

    [Explanation]

11. **In what way was Hannah similar to her sister?**
    - A They were both expert piano players.
    - B Neither sister was nervous.
    - C Both sisters had spent a great deal of time practicing.
    - D Both sisters were nervous at the recital.

    [Compare-and-Contrast]

12. **The author writes that the "piano looked as if it could open its lid and eat her" to show that Hannah**
    - A Was afraid
    - B Hated music
    - C Was hungry
    - D Would play piano

    Pulling-It-Together

13. **How did Hannah feel about Mary being nervous?**
    - A She was comforted that her sister was also scared.
    - B She was embarrassed by her sister's nervousness.
    - C She was ashamed in front of all her friends.
    - D She vowed never again to play with Mary.

    Specific Detail

14. **Which best describes Hannah's feelings towards Mary?**
    - A Jealousy and dislike
    - B Fondness and love
    - C Embarrassment and unease
    - D Fear and anger

    Pulling-It-Together

15. **The next time Mary participates in a recital at Mrs. Johnson's studio, she will most likely**
    - A Practice before her performance
    - B Eat a large meal before leaving home
    - C Go to bed early the night before
    - D Wear different clothing than her sister does

    Prediction

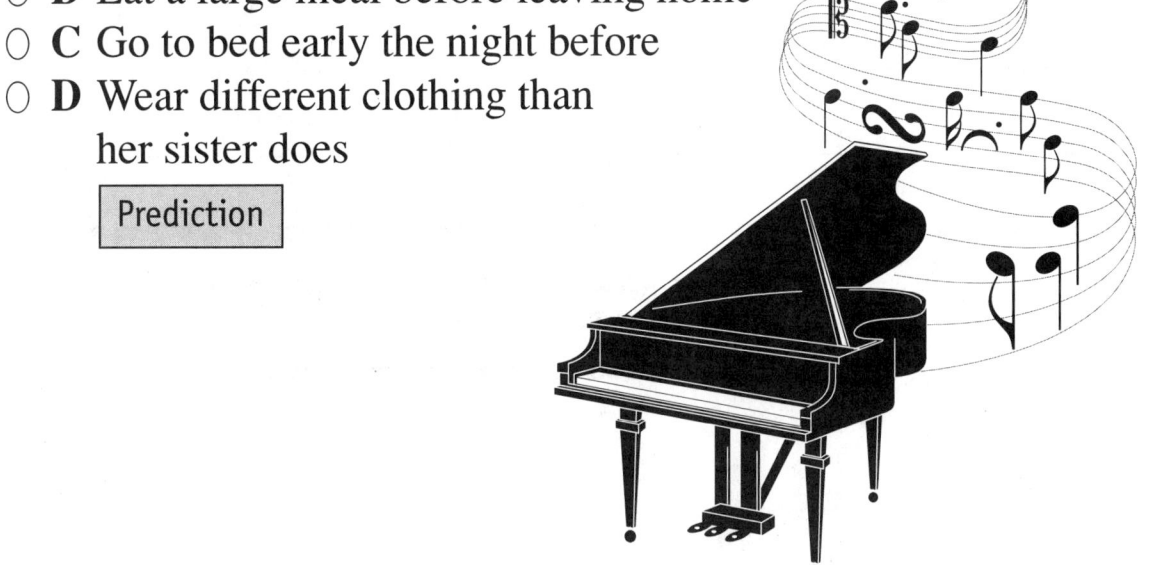

EXTENDED-RESPONSE QUESTION

16. What is the main lesson of the story? Use details from the story to support your answer.

END OF SESSION 2

UNIT 4: WRITING

📕 **Chapter 13:** The Elements of Good Writing

📕 **Chapter 14:** Responding to a Writing Prompt

📕 **Chapter 15:** Writing a Narrative Essay

📕 **Chapter 16:** Writing an Expository Essay

📕 **Chapter 17:** Writing a Persuasive Essay

> This unit will prepare you for the **Grade 3 ISAT Writing Test.** The writing test is usually given in one session, lasting 45 minutes. You will be asked to write one of three types of essays — either a narrative, expository, or persuasive essay.

INTRODUCTION TO WRITING

This unit will introduce you to the tools you need to write well. Before we look at what it takes to be a good writer, let's see what *you* think is needed to write well.

THINK ABOUT IT

What do you think makes someone a good writer?
_____

When you wrote your answer, you probably followed two steps:

★ First, you had to think about what you wanted to say.

★ Second, you had to express your thoughts in words.

Good writers write clearly so that readers understand the thoughts they are expressing. A reader should be able to picture in his or her mind the same thoughts the writer was trying to express.

The writer is able to write down his thoughts in a way that his reader can picture the same thoughts.

Chapter 13

THE ELEMENTS OF GOOD WRITING

In the first part of this book you learned how to become a better reader. In this unit, you will learn how to become a better writer. When you read, you try to understand the writer's ideas. When you write, you try to communicate your own ideas to the reader.

In order to communicate well, your writing should have four important qualities. These four qualities are known as the *elements of good writing*.

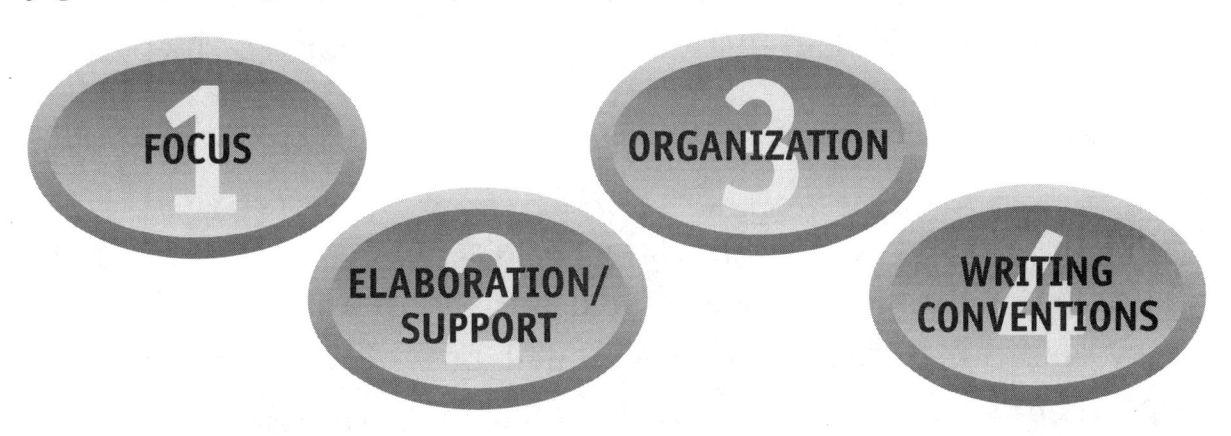

1. **FOCUS**
2. **ELABORATION/ SUPPORT**
3. **ORGANIZATION**
4. **WRITING CONVENTIONS**

On the **Grade 3 ISAT Writing Test,** you will receive a separate score for focus, elaboration/support, and organization. You will also receive a score for your writing conventions. This chapter will explain each of these elements of good writing.

THE WRITING PROMPT

On the writing test, you will be given a writing prompt. A **prompt** is something that encourages you to think. It causes you to respond in some way. The writing prompt on the **Grade 3 ISAT Writing Test** will be divided into two parts:

★ **First Part.** An introductory statement will give background to the writing assignment. For example, the introduction may describe a situation you will have to write about.

★ **Second Part.** The directions will provide a specific writing assignment or task. These directions will tell you:

(1) the essay type you are expected to write — narrative, expository, or persuasive.

(2) the assignment or task you are expected to complete.

Below is a sample prompt similar to one you might find on the writing test. Let's look at this sample prompt and each of its parts:

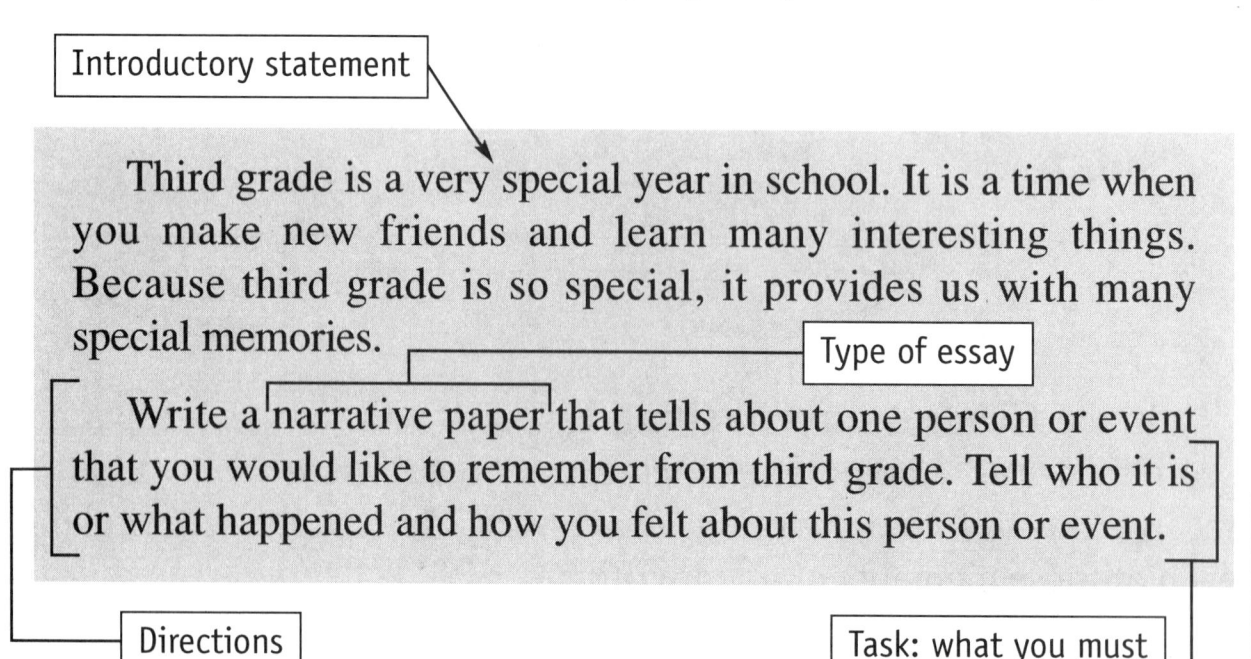

Introductory statement

> Third grade is a very special year in school. It is a time when you make new friends and learn many interesting things. Because third grade is so special, it provides us with many special memories.
>
> Write a narrative paper that tells about one person or event that you would like to remember from third grade. Tell who it is or what happened and how you felt about this person or event.

Type of essay

Directions

Task: what you must write about

Now you know what the prompt on the writing test will look like. Let's look more closely at the four elements of good writing.

FOCUS

Focus means your writing should stay on the task you are expected to answer. Choose a specific topic based on the directions in the writing prompt. Then stick to that topic. Everything in your essay should be focused on answering the task. Do not include unrelated information. For example, you might respond to the prompt on the previous page by writing about an interesting project you did in third grade. Everything in that essay should relate to that project.

ELABORATION / SUPPORT

Elaboration/Support refers to the details and examples you use to support or explain your main idea or position taken in responding to the task in the prompt.

- ★ **When You Explain Something.** If you are explaining something, give specific facts, details, and examples to support each part of your explanation. Put yourself in your reader's shoes. Think about what your reader needs to know to understand what you are explaining. Be sure to include those details.

- ★ **When You Narrate or Describe.** If you are telling about an experience or event, expand your thoughts by describing each event in detail. Tell about the *who, what, when, where, how,* and *why* of each event. Be as specific as you can.

- ★ **When You Take a Position on an Issue.** When you take a position on an issue, give reasons for taking that position. For each reason, list or describe specific facts, details, and examples that explain or support that reason.

ORGANIZATION

Organization, the third element of good writing, refers to how well you put your ideas together. Imagine someone who built a house with the roof at the bottom and the basement on top. The house would surely soon collapse!

In the same way, your essay on the ISAT Writing Test has to be put together in a *logical* and *orderly way*. If your organization is not logical, your reader will not be able to follow what you are writing about.

Your answer on the writing test should be organized into three main parts.

THE INTRODUCTION

When we first meet someone, we introduce ourselves. Similarly, your essay should begin with an introduction where you tell your reader what you are writing about. It is here that you focus on presenting the task or position taken in response to the directions of the prompt. From your introduction, your reader will know at the start what to expect in the rest of your essay.

THE BODY OF YOUR WRITING

The body is the main part of your essay answer. Here is where you focus on giving details and examples to support the task or position taken in the introduction. Be as descriptive as possible. Use all five senses in describing things. Include plenty of details and examples to help your reader understand your ideas.

Within the body of your essay, be sure to organize your ideas and details in some logical order. This makes it easy for the reader to follow your ideas. How you organize your writing will depend on what you are writing about. There are four main ways that good writers use to put their writing in logical order:

★ **Time Order.** If you are telling about an event or experience, the first paragraph should include an umbrella statement identifying the entire experience you are going to write about. Then tell about things in more detail in the order in which they happened. Start by telling about the first event. Describe the event by telling about the *who, what, when, where, how,* and *why.* Then move on to the second event. Proceed in time order until you completely describe all the events that made up the experience.

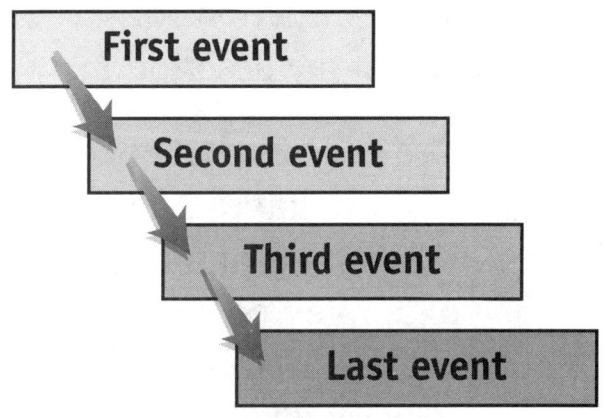

★ **Cause-and-Effect Order.** If you are explaining the causes and effects of an important event, one way is to begin by describing all of the causes. After you have described the causes of the event, then describe the event's effects. Another way to write about causes and effects is to describe each cause and its particular effects, one at a time.

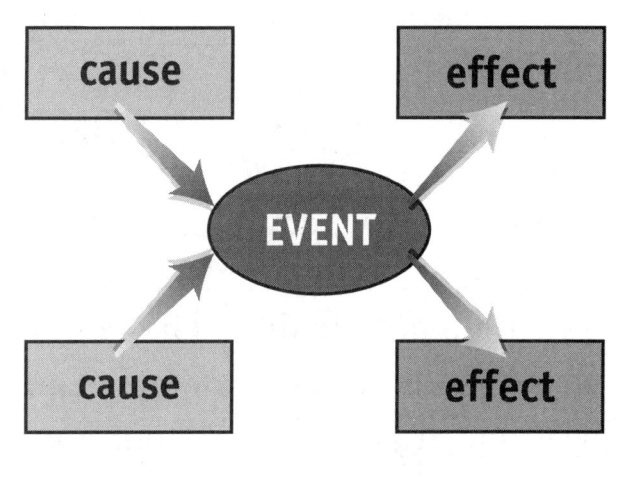

★ **Space Order.** If you are describing an object or scene in your writing, imagine the object or scene in your mind. Then pick some point and begin to describe it. Move left to right, or up and down as you continue your description. Be sure to continue in the same direction for the rest of the description.

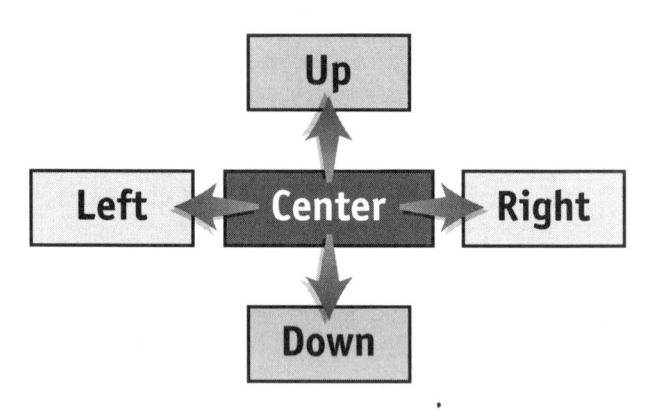

★ **Order of Importance.** If you have a main idea and a number of examples or supporting details, give the general or main idea first. Then provide the supporting details in order of their importance. Give the most important example or reason first. You can also start with the least important first, and move to the most important.

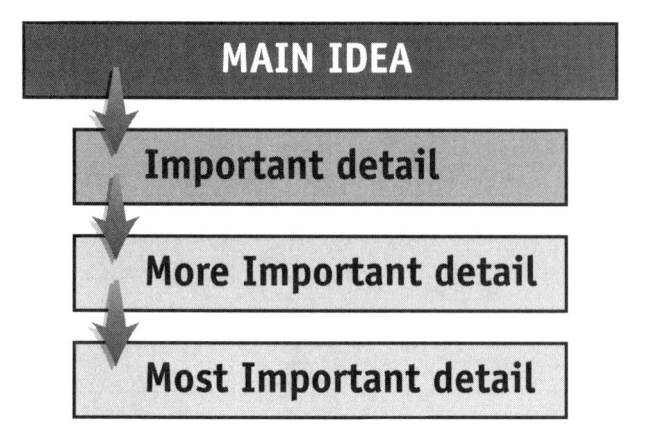

CONCLUSION

When we leave someone, we normally say good-bye. At the end of your essay, you should similarly say good-bye to your reader by writing a conclusion. The conclusion signals to the reader that the writing is coming to an end. There are many ways to conclude your writing. In your conclusion, you may want to briefly summarize the main ideas of the body of your writing. You may also want to state some general moral or lesson that can be learned from what you have written.

A NOTE ABOUT TRANSITION WORDS

An important part of organizing your writing is to use <u>transition words</u>. Transition words act as signposts for your readers. These words tell your readers that you are moving from one point to another. When readers see these signposts, they know they are moving in the right direction. Some useful transition words and phrases include:

★ When giving a list of points, use number words like <u>first</u>, <u>second</u>, and <u>third</u>. Each time the reader sees a new number, he or she will know that you have moved to a new idea or new point.

★ When telling about events, you can often use the day of the week or time of year as a transition. Other useful transitions include <u>the next day</u>, <u>the following week</u>, <u>later that year</u>, and <u>next</u>.

★ Other common transition words include: <u>for example</u>, <u>therefore</u>, <u>also</u>, <u>in addition</u>, <u>another</u>, and <u>then</u>.

WRITING CONVENTIONS

The fourth element of good writing is known as **writing conventions.** Writing conventions are rules that have been developed for standard spelling, grammar, capitalization, and punctuation. The *Handbook of Writing Conventions* in the **Appendix** at the back of this book explains how to avoid several major errors often made by third graders.

CHAPTER 14

RESPONDING TO A WRITING PROMPT

In the last chapter you learned about the basic elements of good writing. Now let's turn our attention to how you can best respond to a writing prompt to produce your best written answer.

STEPS IN RESPONDING TO A WRITING PROMPT

There are four main steps in responding to the writing prompt on the **Grade 3 ISAT Writing Test:**

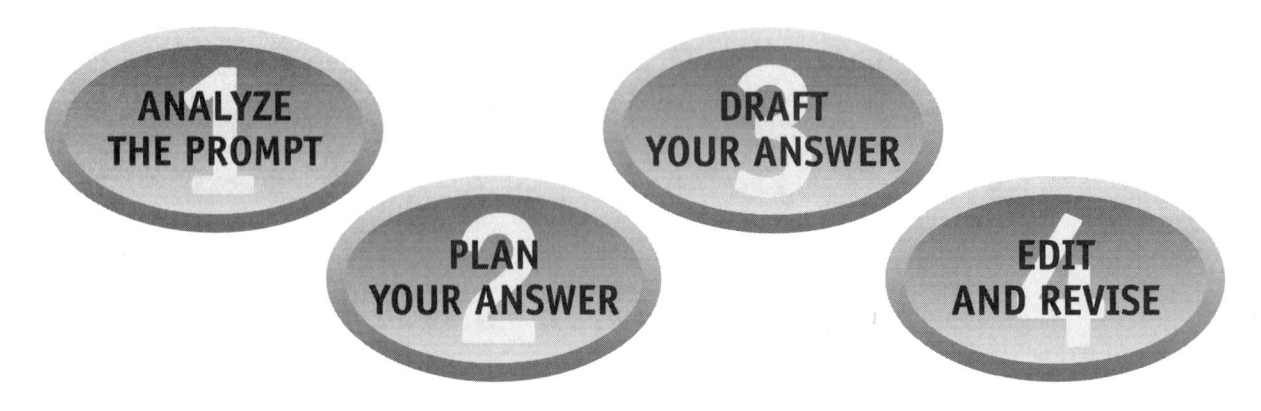

1. **ANALYZE THE PROMPT**
2. **PLAN YOUR ANSWER**
3. **DRAFT YOUR ANSWER**
4. **EDIT AND REVISE**

STEP 1: ANALYZE THE PROMPT

As you know, the **ISAT Writing Test** will present you with a writing prompt.

CHAPTER 14: RESPONDING TO A WRITING PROMPT   139

> The **first paragraph** of the writing prompt will describe a situation or provide background to the writing assignment.

> The **second paragraph** of the writing prompt will have specific directions on what you should write about. This assignment provides a focus for your writing.

Let's look at a sample prompt:

> **WRITING PROMPT**
>
> Your family is deciding what to do this weekend. Some family members want to go to the movies. Other members would like to have a picnic. Do you think your family should go the movies or on a picnic?
>
> Write a persuasive paper telling whether you think the family should go to the movies or have a picnic. Give reasons why you think as you do.

To analyze this prompt, you should use the following steps:

★ First, you must determine the type of writing you are being asked to create. In the sample prompt, are you giving an explanation, writing a persuasive essay, or describing a personal experience?

> *The first sentence of the second paragraph of the prompt tells you that you are being asked to write a persuasive essay.*

★ Examine the question words or commands in the prompt. Does the prompt ask you to ***tell about, explain how, explain why,*** or ***give reasons why***? In the sample prompt, you have to try to persuade your family to agree with your position.

In this sample prompt, you are asked to give reasons why you think as you do.

★ Now take a moment to think about the task in the writing prompt. Use the hints or clues provided in the prompt to spur your thinking.

In this sample prompt, your task is to tell whether you think the family should go to the movies or have a picnic.

STEP 2: PLAN YOUR ANSWER

The next step in the writing process is to **plan** your answer. For many students, this the hardest part of responding to a writing prompt. You need to think of what you want to write about. One way to get ideas is to jot down notes on different items you might write about. Then look them over to see what best responds to the directions in the prompt.

After you select your main idea or have made a choice, start to fill in the details. It sometimes helps to create an **outline** or **topic map** to organize your thoughts about the task in the prompt. You already learned about topic maps in **Chapter 2.** Put your topic in the middle of the paper. Surround this topic with supporting ideas, facts, and examples. Then number your points in the order you want to present them.

Another method is to outline your answer in the form of a hamburger.

★ The **top bun** serves as your *introduction.*

★ The **patties of meat** form the *body of your answer.*

★ The **bottom bun** is your *conclusion.*

The top bun serves as the place where you identify the event you are describing, your main idea, or the position you are taking in response to the prompt.

The patties of meat make up the body of your essay. Here you list reasons, specific details, and examples to support the main idea you stated in the introduction.

The bottom bun serves as the place where you summarize your main ideas and remind the reader of your strongest points.

STEP 3: DRAFT YOUR ANSWER

In this third step of responding to a writing prompt, you turn your hamburger, concept map or other form of prewriting into a finished product. Turn each point of your plan into one or more complete sentences.

Whatever form of prewriting or planning you use, remember to organize your writing into the three parts of an essay — *introduction, body,* and *conclusion.* Also make sure the body of your essay is logically organized and stays focused on the task or writing assignment.

STEP 4: REVISE AND EDIT YOUR ANSWER

The first person to read your writing should be **YOU** — *not* the person who is grading your writing. Always read over your work before you hand it in.

Read your written draft silently to yourself. Pretend you are someone else, reading it for the very first time. Make sure that you have included all your major ideas.

As you review what you have written, ask yourself some questions. If your answer is "no" to any of the following questions, your answer is not finished and needs further work:

> ★ Have you written the *type of essay* — *narrative, expository,* or *persuasive* — required by the writing prompt?
>
> ★ Did you *follow the directions* in the writing prompt?
>
> ★ Does your writing have a *focus*?
>
> ★ Have you *stayed on the topic*?
>
> ★ Do you have an *introduction, body,* and *conclusion*?
>
> ★ Does the body of your essay have a *logical organization*?
>
> ★ Have you *provided details, examples,* and *reasons* to support or explain your position or main idea?
>
> ★ *Could a person reading your paper for the first time understand what you mean?*

Revise your draft by rewriting any sections that are poorly organized. Add ideas and details you may have left out. Take out any extra information that does not relate to the topic or theme of your writing.

On the **Grade 3 ISAT Writing Test,** your final work will be treated as a "first draft." You can just cross out the sections you want to take out, or add words or sentences using arrows.

Also edit your writing by checking for errors in writing conventions. Watch out for mistakes in spelling, grammar, punctuation, and usage.

CHAPTER 15

WRITING A NARRATIVE ESSAY

The **Grade 3 ISAT Writing Test** is given in one session of 40 minutes. The test booklet will have one writing prompt and four lined pages for you to write your answer. You will have to create one of three types of writings — a narrative, expository, or persuasive essay.

On the test, you will **NOT** have a choice of what type of essay to write. The test will only ask you to write one type. Other people in your class may be asked to write another type of essay.

The next three chapters will look at each type of essay you may have to write for the test. This chapter will look at the first type — *a narrative essay.*

WHAT IS A NARRATIVE ESSAY?

To *narrate* means to *tell about* an event or series of related events. A narrative essay therefore tells about an experience or event. On the **Grade 3 ISAT Writing Test,** the prompt may require you to tell about an experience you had and how you felt and reacted. A different prompt may require you to tell about an event you saw and how people in that event reacted.

You may feel somewhat uncomfortable writing about your own experiences. Remember, the purpose of the test is **not** to find out about the details of your personal life. Your teacher is **not** concerned with your actual experiences, but with your ability to write about them.

Let's take a look at a sample writing prompt for a narrative essay:

> **WRITING PROMPT**
>
> One of the fun activities in life is visiting interesting places. When we visit an interesting place, we get to experience and learn about new things.
>
> Write a narrative paper telling about a visit you had to an interesting place.

HINTS FOR WRITING A NARRATIVE ESSAY

When you write a narrative essay, you will be graded on how well you *focus, elaborate, organize,* and use *writing conventions* in your answer. Let's use these four elements as guides to help you write this kind of essay.

FOCUS

The **focus** of your essay will found in the directions of the prompt. The directions will tell you to write about some kind of experience you had or saw. In the sample writing prompt above, you are asked to write about a visit you had to an interesting place. Therefore, your first task is to:

> *Select an experience you have had while visiting an interesting place.*

To choose a good experience to write about, begin by first thinking about all the interesting places that you have visited. You may have visited an interesting place on a family trip, when you went to a museum or ballpark, or even on a walk around the block.

Brainstorm as many of these experiences as you can think of. People often brainstorm in groups, but you can do the same thing on your own. When you *brainstorm*, you jot down any ideas that come into your head, even if some of them do not seem very good. Afterwards, you review the list you created to see which ideas are really good.

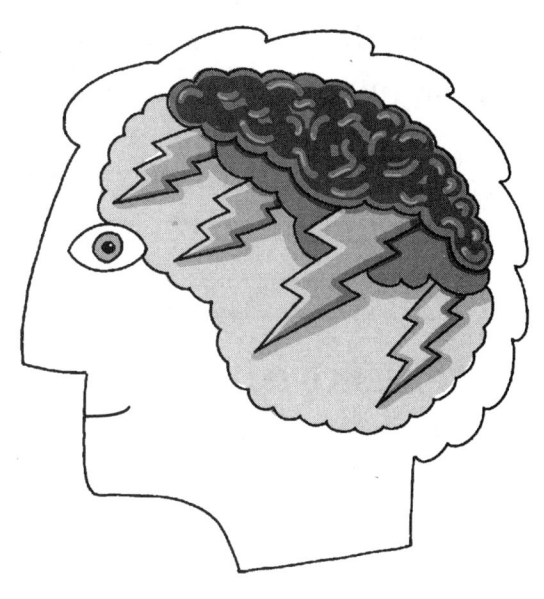

The ideas you come up with will supply the information you will need to write your essay. Now fill the graphic that follows for the sample writing prompt.

List some visits you have made to interesting places.

1.

2.

3.

4.

From the list you just created, choose the place where you feel you had the most interesting experiences to write about:

> ***The place I had the most interesting experiences was:***
> _____

Remember: Once you choose an experience to write about, everything you write in your essay should relate in some way to that experience.

ELABORATION

In a narrative essay, you will have to tell about something that has happened. You must provide details to describe and explain the event you have chosen. These details will help your reader to make a mental picture of what you are writing about.

Think about the question words you learned in Chapter 2. When you describe something, you need to supply the **who, what, where, when,** and **how.** Think about all five senses in describing something. You should also tell how the experience you are writing about has affected you.

The *topic map* on the top of the next page can help you to organize your thoughts when writing a narrative essay. It will help you to remember details of the experience you are writing about.

CHAPTER 15: WRITING A NARRATIVE ESSAY 147

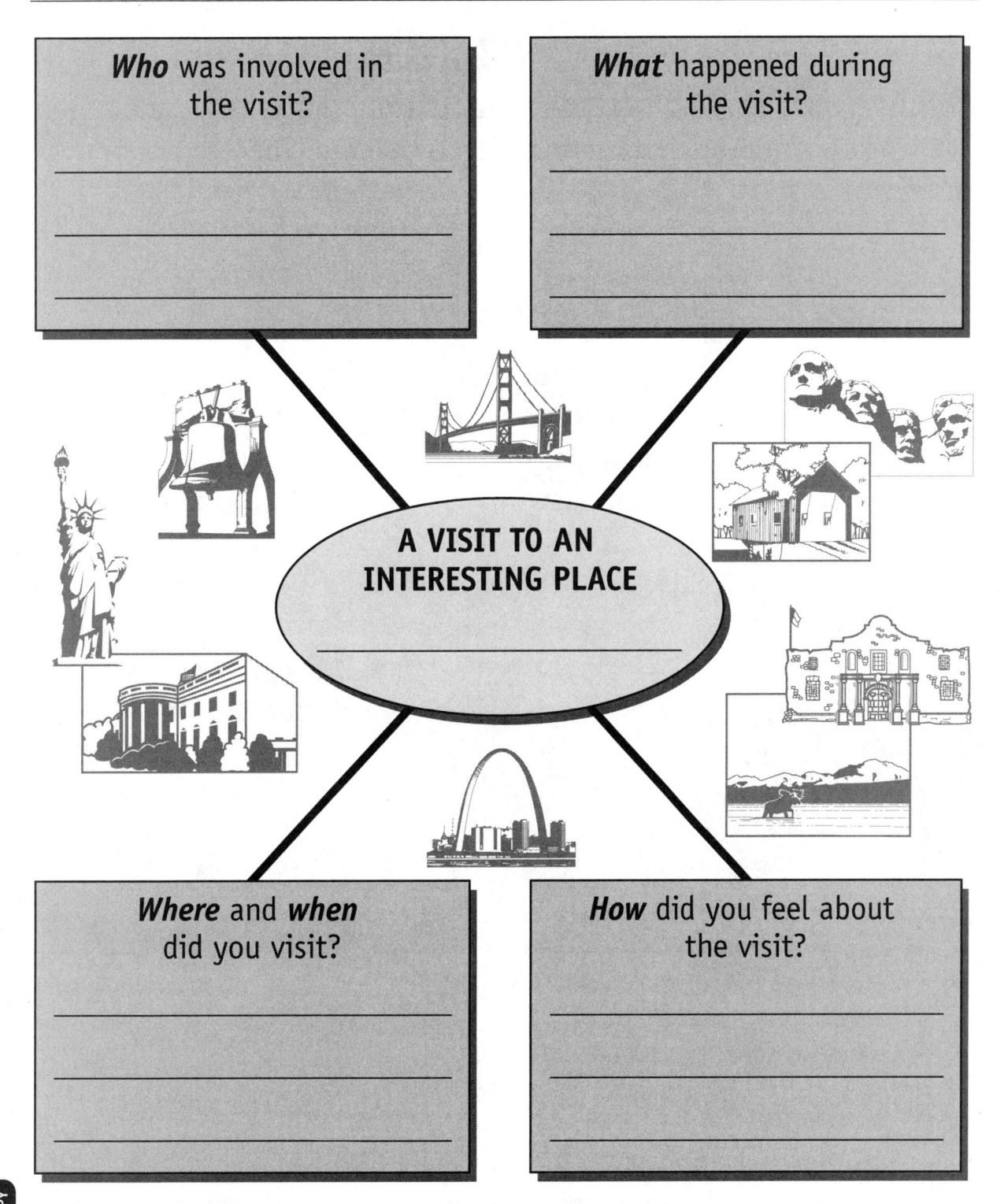

Who was involved in the visit?
_____
_____
_____

What happened during the visit?
_____
_____
_____

A VISIT TO AN INTERESTING PLACE
_____

Where and **when** did you visit?
_____
_____
_____

How did you feel about the visit?
_____
_____
_____

The information you jot down in this topic map will become the body of your essay. Now take the visit you selected on page 146. Put that visit in the center of the topic map above. Then fill out the rest of the boxes with details about that experience.

ORGANIZATION

Be sure your essay has a clear introduction, body, and conclusion. Let's briefly review the organization of each of these parts of your answer:

INTRODUCTION

★ The introduction should identify the place you had the interesting experience and have decided to write about in responding to the prompt. This introduction provides the focus for the rest of your narrative essay.

BODY

★ A narrative essay is usually organized in *time order*. You tell about an event or series of events in the order in which they happen.

★ To help you organize your writing, it may help to take your topic map (see page 147) and number the points in the order you want to introduce them in your essay.

CONCLUSION

★ Restate your opening statement.

★ You may want to say something about how the event you are writing about affected you or led to important changes in your life. For example, did you learn anything important on your visit? Did it leave you with any happy memories that you still cherish?

USEFUL TRANSITION WORDS

Narrative essays are usually organized in time order. The following transition words are often useful:

- ★ At five o'clock, . . .
- ★ On Monday, . . .
- ★ That Summer, . . .
- ★ An hour later, ...
- ★ The next morning, . . .
- ★ Next, then, finally

WRITING CONVENTIONS

After you have finished writing your essay, edit and revise your work. Check your essay for any errors in writing conventions. Be careful to avoid errors in grammar, usage, capitalization, punctuation, and spelling.

A MODEL NARRATIVE ESSAY

The essay on the next page is a sample answer that one student wrote about a visit to an interesting place. As you read this essay, pay particular attention to the suggestions in the boxes alongside the essay.

This paragraph introduces the topic of the essay.	Last summer my family took a trip to Disney World in Orlando, Florida. It was the most exciting and fun visit of my entire life.
These paragraphs give details about Florida and Disney World by telling *who*, *what*, *when* and *where* of the event.	Florida is such an interesting place. The weather was very hot. There were palm trees everywhere. Many of the buildings and hotels were painted bright pink. The first afternoon we arrived in Florida we took it easy. We drove to a beach and went swimming. The next day we went to Disney World. It is a huge place with several different theme parks. In the "Magic Kingdom" we shook hands with Mickey Mouse and Donald Duck. My favorite ride was the Pirates of the Caribbean. I felt a lump in my stomach as we plunged into the darkness. We enjoyed eating all kinds of tasty and different foods.
The last paragraph ends with a conclusion.	I have visited lots of interesting places. I love the Museum of Science and Technology in Chicago, but the most interesting trip I ever went on was to Disney World. The interesting rides, meeting cartoon characters, and the sunny weather made for many happy memories.

PRACTICE WRITING A NARRATIVE ESSAY

Now it's your turn. Use your notes from the topic map you completed earlier in this chapter to write a narrative essay about a visit you had to an interesting place. Remember, you can have an interesting visit in your own neighborhood or somewhere far away.

CHAPTER 15: WRITING A NARRATIVE ESSAY   151

Introduction identifies your selection in response to the task mentioned in the prompt.

Body of your answer comes from the topic map. Give details about the visit in the order that they happened. Remember to use transition words.

Conclusion.

When you have finished writing your essay, revise and edit your work. Remember, you are not finished until you have re-read what you wrote and have made any needed corrections.

Practice Exercises

Directions: Read the writing prompt below:

> **WRITING PROMPT**
>
> Sometimes we accomplish things that we are very proud of. A person might be proud of reading a new book, getting a high score in a video game, or being a real help at home.
>
> Write a narrative paper telling about an accomplishment of which you are proud. Tell what you did and why you feel proud about it.

First, list a series of accomplishments you are proud of.

1.

2.

3.

4.

Select **one** accomplishment you wish to write about: _____

Use the topic map on the next page to supply the necessary details and examples you will need to support your essay.

Chapter 15: Writing a Narrative Essay

What was the accomplishment?
_____
_____

When did it happen?
_____
_____

AN ACCOMPLISHMENT YOU ARE PROUD OF
_____

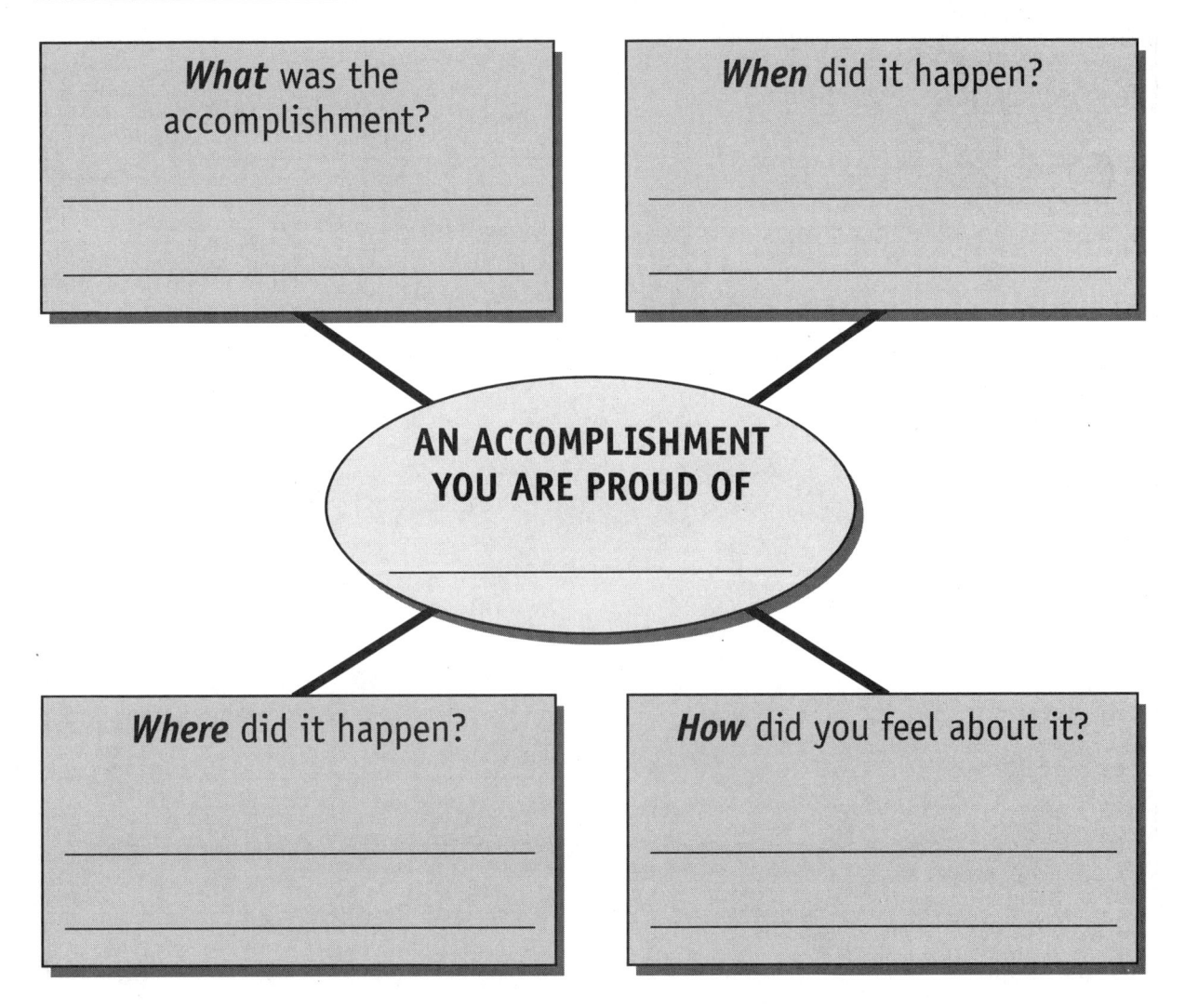

Where did it happen?
_____
_____

How did you feel about it?
_____
_____

Use the blank paper below and on the next page to write your narrative essay.

When you finish writing your essay, revise and edit your work. Remember, you are not finished until you have re-read what you wrote.

CHAPTER 16

WRITING AN EXPOSITORY ESSAY

On the **Grade 3 ISAT Writing Test** you may have to write an expository essay. Let's begin by looking at what an expository essay is.

WHAT IS AN EXPOSITORY ESSAY?

An **expository essay** explains or describes something to your reader. To *explain* means to "make plain or understandable." To *describe* means to write about the features or qualities of something.

On the **Grade 3 ISAT Writing Test,** the prompt may ask you to *explain why* or *how something happened.* A different type of prompt may ask you to *explain why you made a choice.* A third type of prompt may ask you to *describe something.*

Let's look at what you have to do for each of these types of expository essays:

★ To *explain why* something happened, you need to identify the causes that made it happen.

★ To *explain why* you made a choice, first state your choice. Then give the reasons why you made that choice.

★ To **explain how** something happened, you must *explain the way in which it happened*. For example, to **explain how** someone made an important decision, you need to:

(1) *identify* the problem the person faced;

(2) *list the choices* the person had;

(3) *describe steps* the person went through in making the decision.

★ To **describe** something, tell about its qualities. For example, to **describe** a favorite place, first identify that place. Then tell about its climate, how it looks, and what you can do there.

Let's take a look at a sample writing prompt for an expository essay:

> **WRITING PROMPT**
>
> In our lives, we come into contact with many different kinds of people. Sometimes we come across someone who has a great influence on our life. This person influences how we think, feel, or act.
>
> Write an expository paper explaining how someone has been important in your life. Show the ways in which that person has influenced you. Explain each way.

HINTS FOR WRITING AN EXPOSITORY ESSAY

As we did in the last chapter for writing a narrative essay, let's use *focus, support, organization* and the *use of writing conventions* as guides.

FOCUS

The **focus** of your expository essay will be provided by the directions of the prompt. The directions will tell you to explain or describe something. In the sample prompt on the previous page, the directions told you to write about how a person has influenced you.

Your first task is to select that person. It could be a parent, friend, or anyone else you have known. One simple way of selecting that person is to make a list of those people who are most important to you. Remember, the person you choose will provide the focus of what you write. Now complete the list below.

List some people who are important to you.

1.

2.

3.

Select **one** person from the list who has had a great influence on your life:

A person who has had a great influence on my life is:

Once you choose a person to write about, everything you write in your essay should relate to that person and how that person has influenced you.

SUPPORT

In an expository essay, you have to provide details to support your main points. In the sample prompt, you have to *explain how* someone has influenced you. This means you have to give facts and examples that show how this person has influenced you. The graphic organizer below will help you to organize your thoughts. It requires you to come up with particular details and examples you can use to support your essay.

Identify the Person:	Describe the Person:

Ways That Person Has Influenced You:

(1)

(2)

(3)

The information you jot down in the graphic organizer above will become the basis of your answer. Start with the person you chose. Put that person's name in the box on the left. Next, describe him or her in the box on the right. Then fill out the bottom box with details about the person and how he or she has influenced you.

ORGANIZATION

Let's briefly review the organization of your essay:

INTRODUCTION

★ The introduction provides the focus for the rest of your expository essay. In the case of our sample writing prompt, the introduction should identify a person who has had an influence on you.

★ You can follow this by briefly stating each way the person influenced you. Then provide a transition sentence to the body of your essay.

BODY

★ Organize your essay in some logical order — time, space, or order of importance. An expository essay is often organized by order of importance. You might list the most important reason first. For the sample prompt, you have to show the ways the person you selected has influenced you.

★ Begin by telling the most important way the person has influenced you. Use another paragraph to show a second way this person has influenced you.

CONCLUSION

★ Restate your opening statement. You might summarize how the person brought about important changes in your life.

> **USEFUL TRANSITION WORDS**
>
> Often an expository essay presents several points in order of importance. Some useful transition words and phrases for expository essays include:
>
> ★ The first way, the second way, the last way
>
> ★ The first reason, the second reason, the third reason
>
> ★ One way, a second way, the next way
>
> ★ In addition, another, also

WRITING CONVENTIONS

In the final step, edit and revise your work. Check your essay for any errors in grammar, usage, capitalization, punctuation, and spelling.

A MODEL EXPOSITORY ESSAY

The essay on the next page is a sample showing what one student wrote in response to the writing prompt about someone who has influenced him. Pay particular attention to the suggestions in the boxes alongside the essay.

Chapter 16: Writing an Expository Essay

> The first part of the introduction identifies and describes Mr. Smith — the person selected in response to the prompt.

> This sentence briefly previews two ways Mr. Smith influenced the writer.

One of the most important people in my life was Mr. Smith, my third grade teacher. He had dark brown hair. His smile showed his willingness to help others. I will never forget him, because he influenced my life in so many ways. He made me feel welcome, gave me a sense of pride, and helped me to make friends.

> Here the writer explains ways Mr. Smith influenced his life.

One way Mr. Smith influenced me was by making me feel welcome to the United States. I was a new student from China. When I first arrived here, everything was strange and different. I did not always feel welcome, but Mr. Smith went out of his way to let me know I was important.

A second way Mr. Smith influenced me was by helping me make friends. I did not speak English well. This made me very shy and uncomfortable whenever I would meet someone new. At playtime or lunch, Mr. Smith always brought over other students and introduced me to them. That is how I met my best friend, Adrian.

I learned many important lessons in Mr. Smith's class. He taught me to have confidence in myself and not to be afraid of meeting new people. I will always remember Mr. Smith, no matter how old I get.

> The conclusion summarizes how Mr. Smith has had a lasting influence on the writer.

PRACTICE WRITING AN EXPOSITORY ESSAY

Now it's your turn. Use your notes from the topic map you completed earlier in this chapter to write an expository essay about a person in your life who has influenced you.

Introduction comes from your notes on the focus selection.

Body of your answer comes from the notes in your graphic organizer.

Conclusion.

CHAPTER 16: WRITING AN EXPOSITORY ESSAY

When you have finished writing your essay, revise and edit your work. Remember, you are not finished until you have re-read what you wrote and have made any needed corrections.

Practice Exercises

Directions: Read the writing prompt below:

> **WRITING PROMPT**
> We all have favorite things we like to study and do. What is your favorite subject in school?
>
> Write an expository paper telling about your favorite subject in school. Give the reasons why it is your favorite subject.

Now complete the list below.

List some of your favorite subjects.

1.

2.

3.

Select **one** subject that is your favorite in school.

My favorite subject in school is:

Use the graphic organizer below to help you think of details and examples you will need to support your essay.

Identify the Subject:	Describe the Subject:

Reasons Why This Subject Is Your Favorite:
(1)
(2)
(3)

Use the blank paper on this and the following page to write your expository essay.

When you finish, revise and edit your essay. After you have checked your essay and are satisfied with it, you are finished.

CHAPTER 17

WRITING A PERSUASIVE ESSAY

On the **Grade 3 ISAT Writing Test,** you may be asked to write a persuasive essay. Let's begin by looking at what a persuasive essay is.

WHAT IS A PERSUASIVE ESSAY?

A **persuasive essay** seeks to convince the reader to adopt the writer's point of view. To persuade means to get another person to do or to believe something. A persuasive essay tries to get the reader to support a position or take some action.

Let's take a look at a sample writing prompt for a persuasive essay:

WRITING PROMPT

Your school is considering inviting a fast-food restaurant to provide school lunches. Should your school be permitted to serve fast-food lunches to students? Why or why not?

Write a persuasive paper telling whether you think your school should invite a fast-food restaurant to provide school lunches. Give reasons why you feel as you do.

HINTS FOR WRITING A PERSUASIVE ESSAY

As with narrative and expository essays, we can use *focus, support, organization,* and the use of *writing conventions* as guides for writing this type of essay.

FOCUS

The **focus** of your essay will be provided by the directions in the prompt. The prompt will ask you to take a position on some question or issue. For example, the sample prompt asks you to take a stand on whether your school should invite a fast-food restaurant to provide school lunches. Should your school serve fast-food lunches or not?

Your first task is to decide what position to take on the issue presented in the prompt. One way to decide what position to take is to make a list of reasons in favor of each side. Try to think of all the advantages that would occur if either position were adopted. Also think of the disadvantages of each position.

In Favor of Fast-food School Lunches	Opposed to Fast-food School Lunches
1. Students enjoy fast foods and will eat more of their lunches.	1. Fast food is not very healthy for students.
2. Some parents do not have time to prepare lunch for their children.	2. Having fast food in school sets the wrong example for many students.
3. Now you add a reason: _____	3. Now you add a reason: _____

Once you have completed your list of reasons for each side of the issue, you have to select your **position.** You will state your position in the introduction of your essay. Your position is the side of the issue that you support. It will serve as the focus of your persuasive essay.

> *Select the position you support on the issue of serving fast-food lunches in school.*
>
> *MY POSITION IS:* _____

SUPPORT

Now you have to support your position with reasons. Stay focused on providing reasons that support your side of the issue. *You should only give the reasons for your own side. Never give the reasons for both sides of an issue in a persuasive essay.* Remember, you are trying to convince the reader to adopt your point of view on this issue.

Each reason that you present in your essay should be explained with examples and facts. After a person reads your essay, he or she should come away believing that your point of view is correct, and want to adopt your point of view. For example, if you believe your school should serve fast-food lunches, you want to convince your reader to adopt the same point of view. You might point out that many of your friends enjoy fast foods. They have said they would eat more of their lunch if fast foods were served.

ORGANIZATION

Like the other types of essays, a persuasive essay needs an introduction, body, and a conclusion. Let's briefly review the organization of each part.

INTRODUCTION

★ The introduction should clearly state to the reader your position on the issue in the prompt.

★ You should briefly state each reason why you favor that position. These reasons are then fully discussed in the body of your essay.

BODY

★ In the body of your essay, give the reasons for your position together with supporting details.

★ Writers usually present their reasons in *order of importance*. You can start with your most important reason first. Another way is to start with the least important reason and end with the most important reason.

★ Use a separate paragraph for each reason you present. The focus of each paragraph should be a discussion of that particular reason.

CONCLUSION

★ Conclude your essay by restating your position on the issue. For the sample prompt, you would restate whether you favor or oppose fast-food school lunches.

★ It is a good idea to briefly summarize the reasons why you think you are right. This concludes your essay with a powerful finish.

> ## USEFUL TRANSITION WORDS
>
> For a persuasive essay, some useful transition words and phrases include:
>
> ★ First, second, third
>
> ★ Therefore, one can see
>
> ★ In conclusion, I feel
>
> ★ The first reason, the second reason, the third reason

WRITING CONVENTIONS

As always, edit and revise your work after you finish writing. Check for errors you may have made in grammar, usage, capitalization, punctuation, and spelling.

A MODEL PERSUASIVE ESSAY

The essay on the next page is a sample answer that one student wrote. He was writing in response to a prompt asking whether his school should invite a fast-food restaurant to provide school lunches.

CHAPTER 17: WRITING A PERSUASIVE ESSAY

> This introduction states your position and gives a preview of the reasons why.

> Here the author previews the main reasons for her position.

My school is considering inviting a fast-food restaurant like McDonalds or Taco Bell to provide school lunches. I oppose fast-food lunches in school. First, fast food is unhealthy. Second, fast-food lunches in school set a bad example for students. Third, fast food lunches would add to the litter problem in school.

The most important reason why I oppose fast-food lunches in school is because fast foods are unhealthy. Fast foods have a lot of fat and salt in them. They are often fried in fat. All of this is unhealthy.

> In the body of the essay, the writer discusses each reason in a separate paragraph with supporting details.

The second reason I would oppose fast-food lunches is because it sets a bad example. Kids often get hooked on fast foods and never learn to appreciate healthy and well-balanced meals. Schools should not encourage this.

The final reason I oppose fast food in school is that it will create too much litter. Students will throw their wrappers and soda cups on the floor. Garbage cans will overflow with all of this added litter.

In conclusion, there are three good reasons why we should not allow our school to serve fast-food lunches. It would be unhealthy, set a bad example for students, and create a litter problem in school.

> The conclusion summarizes the writer's point of view.

172 MASTERING THE GRADE 3 ISAT READING AND WRITING TESTS

PRACTICE
WRITING A PERSUASIVE ESSAY

Use your notes to write a persuasive essay for or against fast-food lunches in school.

State your position. Then preview the reasons for it or make a general statement about fast-food lunches.

Explain the reasons for your position in detail. Use a separate paragraph for each reason you present. Remember, you are trying to convince your reader to adopt your point of view.

Summarize your point of view in your conclusion or provide some other strong persuasive finish.

CHAPTER 17: WRITING A PERSUASIVE ESSAY   173

When you have finished writing your essay, revise and edit your work. Remember, you are not finished until you have re-read what you wrote and made any needed corrections.

Practice Exercises

Directions: Read the writing prompt below:

> **WRITING PROMPT**
>
> Some teachers give homework on weekends. Other teachers feel that weekends should be spent on family activities, sports, and relaxation. They do not assign homework on weekends. Should third-graders be assigned homework on weekends? Why or why not?
>
> Write a persuasive paper telling why or why not you think third-graders should be assigned homework on weekends. Give reasons why you feel as you do.

Try to think of all the advantages and disadvantages if either position were adopted. Use the boxes below and on the next page to supply the reasons you will need to support your essay.

In Favor of Homework on Weekends

1. Reason: _____
   _____

2. Reason: _____
   _____

3. Reason: _____
   _____

Opposed to Homework on Weekends

1. Reason: _____
   _____

2. Reason: _____
   _____

3. Reason: _____
   _____

Now that you have created a list of reasons in favor of each side of the issue, you have to select your position.

Select the position you support on the issue of homework on the weekends.

MY POSITION IS: _____

Use the blank paper below and on the next page to write your persuasive essay.

When you finish, revise and edit your essay. After you have checked your essay and are satisfied with it, you are finished.

CHAPTER 18

A PRACTICE READING TEST

This practice reading test is divided into three sessions.

★ **Session 1** has 14 multiple-choice word analysis questions, and a reading passage with 13 multiple-choice questions.

★ **Session 2** has a reading passage with 19 multiple-choice questions and one extended-response question.

★ **Session 3** also has a reading passage with 19 multiple-choice questions and one extended-response question.

You may look back at the readings as often as you like. Try to time yourself. You will have **40 minutes** to complete each session. Timing yourself will give you an idea of how long it will take you to answer such questions. Good luck.

START OF SESSION 1

WORD ANALYSIS

Directions: Your teacher will read each question and you will mark your answer by darkening in the circle (O) next to the letter of the best answer. All of these questions have only one correct answer.

1. Which word BEGINS with the same sound as *germ*?
   - O **A** good
   - O **B** game
   - O **C** gentle
   - O **D** ghost

2. Which word has the same "c" sound as the letter "c" in *local*?
   - O **A** racing
   - O **B** city
   - O **C** coin
   - O **D** church

3. The men *scrambled* into the bus. Which word BEGINS with the same sounds as *scrambled*?
   - O **A** school
   - O **B** shoe
   - O **C** screen
   - O **D** siren

4. Which word has the same "a" sound as the letter "a" in *stamp*?
   - O **A** hand
   - O **B** star
   - O **C** stake
   - O **D** rain

5. Which word BEGINS with the same sounds as *skill*?
   - A saddle
   - B shell
   - C swing
   - D school

6. Which word has the SAME sound as the letter "o" in *go*?
   - A pot
   - B boy
   - C snow
   - D boots

7. She liked to *watch* her mother. Which word ENDS with the same sound as *watch*?
   - A fudge
   - B fish
   - C switch
   - D wash

8. What does *preview* mean?
   - A to view before
   - B to view again
   - C to view afterwards
   - D unable to view

9. Which word has two syllables?
   - A lollipop
   - B catch
   - C family
   - D decide

10. **What is the ROOT of the word *beautiful*?**
    - A beauty
    - B full
    - C pretty
    - D be

11. **What does *dissatisfied* mean?**
    - A very satisfied
    - B not satisfied
    - C somewhat satisfied
    - D extremely satisfied

Look at the chart and answer the question that follows:

bio = life	geo = earth	ology = study of
astro = space	onomy = study of	metry = to measure

12. **Which subject is concerned with the study of living things?**
    - A geology
    - B astronomy
    - C geometry
    - D biology

13. **What is the PREFIX of the word *misleading*?**
    - A mis
    - B lead
    - C mislead
    - D ing

14. **What does *unbeatable* mean?**
    - A something that can be beaten
    - B something that cannot be beaten
    - C something already beaten
    - D something that will be beaten

CARRIE ROSE HATED RED
by Susan Uhlig

Carrie Rose hated to wear red. She also disliked hot pink, neon green, and electric blue. Carrie Rose thought they made people notice her. And Carrie Rose didn't like being noticed. In fact, she worked at not being noticed. Carrie Rose sat quietly. She colored quietly. She wore quiet shoes. She never raised her hand. Even at lunch Carrie was quiet so that no one would notice her.

But Carrie Rose noticed the others. Ivy always giggled. Juan raised his hand during reading. Emily chased Juan at recess. Carrie Rose wondered if they minded being noticed.

On Friday the teacher took a windup dog out of his desk. He wound it up. The little dog wagged its tail. Carrie Rose almost laughed out loud. "This is Crackers," Mr. Warner said. "He wants to go home with a student each weekend."

Oh! Come to my house, Carrie Rose thought. *You're so cute. I'll show Dad how you wag your tail!*

"Who wants to take Crackers home?" the teacher asked.

Kids near Carrie Rose raised their hands. She had never raised her hand in class. She lifted her hand from her lap to the desktop. Could she raise it higher? Too late. Mr. Warner had chosen somebody else.

CONTINUED

To all the groans, Mr. Warner said, "Don't worry. Everyone will get a turn. I'll choose someone else next Friday."

All weekend Carrie Rose worried about raising her hand. Maybe she needed practice. Maybe she could get used to it. And then on Friday she could raise her hand like the others. On Monday her hand inched up for calendar person. Alex was chosen.

That night in her room, Carrie Rose practiced raising her hand in front of a mirror. It felt silly, but she thought it might help. On Tuesday her hand went halfway up. Mr. Warner called on Carrie Rose to pass out papers. With fingers trembling, Carrie Rose handed out the sheets. Some kids thanked her, others just took the paper. Carrie Rose smiled when she went back to her seat. Passing out papers was fun.

On Wednesday Carrie Rose didn't raise her hand in time to lead the Pledge of Allegiance. On Thursday her hand popped up for line leader. Ivy was chosen. Carrie Rose sighed. On Friday Carrie Rose couldn't sit still. Could she get her hand up in time? Would the teacher choose her?

Finally, Mr. Warner said, "Who wants to take Crackers home?" Carrie Rose's hand leaped straight up. So did everyone else's. She waited. And waited. What was taking so long?

CONTINUED

> "Carrie Rose," Mr. Warner said at last. Smiling, Carrie Rose walked to the front of the room and gently took Crackers.
>
> "You're coming home with me!" she whispered. Carrie Rose still hates to wear red, and she still wears quiet shoes. But now Carrie Rose loves to volunteer for all kinds of things.

15. **Which sentence best summarizes the story?**
    - A Carrie Rose hates to wear the color red.
    - B Carrie Rose does not like to raise her hand.
    - C Carrie Rose overcomes shyness by learning to raise her hand.
    - D Carrie Rose is chosen to take home a mechanical dog.

16. **How was Carrie Rose different from some of her classmates?**
    - A She did not like to be noticed.
    - B She giggled in class.
    - C She raised her hand during reading.
    - D She did not like dogs.

17. **At the start of the story, why did Carrie Rose hate to wear red?**
    - A She thought it would make people notice her.
    - B She thought it did not go with the color of her hair.
    - C Red was not her favorite color.
    - D She preferred to wear hot pink.

18. **Why had Carrie Rose never raised her hand in class before?**
    - A She did not speak English well.
    - B She did not like to be noticed.
    - C She did not want to take "Crackers" home.
    - D She did not know the answers to the teacher's questions.

19. Which event happened first?
    - A Ivy was chosen as line leader.
    - B Carrie Rose practiced raising her hand at home.
    - C Carrie Rose was picked to take Crackers home.
    - D Carrie Rose passed out papers in class.

20. Who was "Crackers"?
    - A A toy dinosaur that belonged to Juan
    - B A pet frog that belonged to Mr. Warner
    - C A new student in the class
    - D A wind-up dog that wagged its tail

21. When Mr. Warner chose someone to take home Crackers, there were *groans*. What are *groans*?
    - A Moans and cries
    - B Shouting and whistling
    - C Smiles and applause
    - D Hand clapping and cheers

22. How did Carrie Rose get used to raising her hand?
    - A She practiced at home in front of a mirror.
    - B She got her friends to help her.
    - C She practiced in front of her parents.
    - D Mr. Warner helped her after school.

23. Why did Mr. Warner let students take Crackers home for the weekend?
    - A It was a reward for students.
    - B It added humor to his class lessons.
    - C It helped Carrie Rose overcome her shyness.
    - D It allowed students to learn about raising animals.

24. What shows that Carrie Rose was nervous as she passed out the papers in her class?
   ○ **A** Her fingers trembled.
   ○ **B** Papers slipped out of her hand as she walked.
   ○ **C** Other kids made fun of her.
   ○ **D** She smiled when she went back to her seat.

25. Why wasn't Carrie Rose chosen by Mr. Warner to lead the Pledge of Allegiance?
   ○ **A** He did it in alphabetical order, and it wasn't her turn.
   ○ **B** She did not volunteer to do it.
   ○ **C** She did not raise her hand in time.
   ○ **D** She did not know how to lead the Pledge of Allegiance.

26. What shows that Mr. Warner was aware of Carrie Rose's efforts to participate in class?
   ○ **A** He spoke to her after class.
   ○ **B** He called her parents.
   ○ **C** He picked her to take home Crackers.
   ○ **D** He chose Ivy to be line leader.

27. What is the main theme of this story?
   ○ **A** A person can overcome problems like shyness.
   ○ **B** Shy people are just like everybody else.
   ○ **C** Teachers can help you overcome all of your problems.
   ○ **D** Volunteering is important in life.

END OF SESSION 1

STOP

HAPPY BIRTHDAY, BASKETBALL!
by Charles Davis

It was the summer of 1891. Born in Canada, James Naismith had just become an instructor at the YMCA Training School in Springfield, Massachusetts. He had been given a challenge by his boss: to invent a new game. It had to be easy to learn and easy to play indoors during the winter. The game couldn't be rough or dangerous. Most important, it had to be fun and played to the highest standards of good sportsmanship.

At first, James tried taking outdoor games the students knew and bringing them indoors. But indoor rugby and soccer were too rough to play in a small gym. People could get hurt. When his students played lacrosse in the gym, they broke the windows. With only a day left before he had to report the new game to his boss, James still hadn't come up with the right game.

James Naismith and his wife stand next to the peach baskets originally used as the game's goals.

So he started thinking. Why not take parts from different games and make a new one? From soccer he chose the large ball. From lacrosse, he took the idea of a goal.

He decided to put the goal up high so it could not be easily defended. From football came the idea of passing the ball to move it down the court.

CONTINUED

As he slept that night, he dreamed up the new game and how it would be played. The next morning, he wrote down thirteen rules. Then he went to look for something to use as goals.

He asked building repairman Pop Stebbins for two boxes, but Pop couldn't find any. "I have two peach baskets in the storeroom; will they do?" Pop said. James took the baskets and tacked them to the jogging track along the gym's ten-foot-high balcony.

As the students entered the gym, James explained the rules to them. He divided the eighteen students into two teams. Then the world's first basketball game got underway. The students had a blast! It was a little confusing at first. Nobody really knew the rules yet. When the game was over, the score was 1-0. All the students could talk about was how much fun the new game was. They decided it needed a name.

The players who played the first game of basketball at the YMCA Training School. Naismith is in a business suit.

"How about Naismith ball," young Frank Mahan suggested. "You invented it, it should have your name." James laughed, saying nobody would play a game called "Naismith ball." Frank responded, "How about basketball?" James agreed.

In the years following that game, basketball has changed in many ways. Bouncing the ball, or "dribbling," was added as another way to move the ball down the court. Peach baskets were replaced with metal baskets, but they still didn't have open bottoms until 1912.

CONTINUED

> Soon the game became the most popular activity at the YMCA. Today, it's one of the world's favorite games. James Naismith would be pleased to see modern players soar through the air for a jam or thread a pass through the lane. But he'd be even happier to see them shaking hands as friends when the game ended.

1. **What is the article mostly about?**
   - A the life of James Naismith
   - B how the game of basketball was invented
   - C the importance of basketball in society
   - D how the game of basketball has changed

2. **The story tells us: The students had a *blast*. What does *blast* mean in this sentence?**
   - A A loud explosion
   - B A sign of danger
   - C An exciting time
   - D A noisy outburst

3. **Basketball is a favorite American sport, but its inventor was born in**
   - A Canada
   - B Massachusetts
   - C Ireland
   - D Mexico

4. **What was the job of Pop Stebbins?**
   - A Athletic director
   - B Coach
   - C Repairman
   - D Teacher

5. **When was the game of basketball invented?**
   - A 1891
   - B 1900
   - C 1912
   - D 1925

6. **Which is a factual statement about the game of basketball?**
   - A Basketball has been played for over 100 years.
   - B Basketball was originally called Naismith ball.
   - C When it was first invented, basketball had no rules.
   - D Basketball has remained unchanged since it was first invented.

7. **What led James Naismith to invent the game of basketball?**
   - A He came up with the game to relieve his boredom.
   - B His boss challenged him to invent a new indoor game.
   - C He hated outdoor winter sports.
   - D His job at the YMCA was to create new sports games.

8. **Which development in the history of basketball took place last?**
   - A Peach baskets were replaced with metal ones.
   - B The baskets were given open bottoms.
   - C Dribbling was added.
   - D The game was named basketball.

9. **What shows that some outdoor sports could NOT be safely played in a small gym?**
   - A Naismith took the idea of a goal from lacrosse.
   - B Outdoor sports were no fun when done indoors.
   - C Outdoor sports have different standards of good sportsmanship.
   - D Rugby and soccer were too rough.

10. **What shows that Naismith borrowed ideas from other games to invent basketball?**
    - A He made the goal high so it could not be easily defended.
    - B He used peach baskets from the repairman.
    - C He took the idea of passing the ball from football.
    - D He divided the students into two groups.

11. **When did Naismith come up with the game of basketball?**
    ○ **A** He thought it up while talking with his boss.
    ○ **B** His students first suggested the idea to him.
    ○ **C** He dreamed of the new game while sleeping.
    ○ **D** He came up with it while watching a game of lacrosse.

12. **Why was Naismith opposed to the name "Naismith ball"?**
    ○ **A** He was embarrassed that others should know his name.
    ○ **B** He felt no one would want to play a game with such a name.
    ○ **C** The name was already being used by another game.
    ○ **D** He wanted credit for having invented the name, not a student.

13. **Why was the first game of basketball a little confusing?**
    ○ **A** There were too many players on each team.
    ○ **B** No one knew the rules of the game yet.
    ○ **C** The baskets were on different sides of the court.
    ○ **D** Dribbling the ball was not allowed.

14. **What happened in basketball before open bottoms were introduced to the baskets in 1912?**
    ○ **A** Someone had to take the ball out of the basket.
    ○ **B** No one was allowed to dribble the ball.
    ○ **C** There was no passing of the ball permitted.
    ○ **D** It was much harder to score a basket.

15. **Why was "dribbling" later added to the game of basketball?**
    ○ **A** To make it easier to score a basket
    ○ **B** To make it safer than passing
    ○ **C** As another way to move the ball on the court
    ○ **D** To make it easier to remove the ball from the net

16. "James Naismith would be pleased to see modern players <u>soar</u> through the air for a jam or thread a pass through the lane." What does the word <u>soar</u> mean?
    - ○ A Rise up
    - ○ B Make noise
    - ○ C Feel pain
    - ○ D Move fast

17. What is the main idea of this article?
    - ○ A Basketball was invented in 1891.
    - ○ B Dribbling was added to basketball after the game was invented.
    - ○ C Naismith invented basketball by taking parts of different outdoor games.
    - ○ D Basketball is one of the world's favorite games.

18. Why did Naismith tack the peach baskets to the ten-foot high lower rail of the gym's balcony jogging track?
    - ○ A He wanted both teams to jump when scoring.
    - ○ B It was the only place to hang the peach baskets.
    - ○ C He put the goals up high to make them difficult to defend.
    - ○ D It would be impossible for a player to damage the baskets.

19. In what way is basketball similar today to when it was first invented?
    - ○ A Fun and sportsmanship are still important parts of the game.
    - ○ B The game remains rough and dangerous.
    - ○ C Players move the ball by dribbling.
    - ○ D The basket consists of a metal hoop and net.

EXTENDED-RESPONSE QUESTION

20. What are two ways the game of basketball has changed since the first game was played? Use information from the passage in your answer.

END OF SESSION 2

TASHIRA'S TURN
edited by William J. Bennett

One day during a lunch break Tashira found her mother in the schoolyard with a bucket of soap and water. She was scrubbing a wall where someone had written some ugly words and pictures. "Mama!" Tashira called. "What are you doing?"

"I'm helping your teachers keep the school clean," her mother said. When Tashira asked if it was hard work, her mother said, "It's nothing. It's just my turn to help, you see."

The school bell rang. Tashira's mom went back to scrubbing the wall. All the ugly words and pictures ran to the ground, where they turned into puddles of silver and gold.

The next day Tashira was walking past her church, when she heard voices in the sky. She looked up and saw her teacher on the roof! "Hello, Mrs. Jenkins," Tashira called. "What're you doing up there?"

"We're helping Reverend Wilburn," her teacher proclaimed. "The steeple needs a fresh coat of paint."

"That's brave of you to climb so high," Tashira shouted.

"Its not so high," her teacher said. "Besides, it's our turn to help."

CONTINUED

The next morning, Tashira was skipping rope when she saw Reverend Wilburn with a basket under his arm.

"Hi, Reverend Wilburn," she called. "Where are you going with that big basket?"

"I'm taking dinner to Officer Hamlette and his family." Reverend Wilburn smiled. "Mrs. Hamlette just had a baby. Everyone in the neighborhood is taking turns bringing her a meal." He lifted the basket's cover so Tashira could peek inside.

"It's so kind of you to cook such a nice, juicy turkey," she said.

"Oh, it's just my turn to help, that's all," said Reverend Wilburn.

The next day Tashira went to the park. The swings were still because a gang of boys were scaring the little children away. Then Officer Hamlette came along. When the bad boys saw him, they ran away. Officer Hamlette stood on the corner watching them go. Before long, all the little children came out to play.

"Thanks, Officer Hamlette," called Tashira. "The little children were scared to play until you came along."

"Oh, its nothing," smiled Officer Hamlette. "It's just my turn to help, that's all."

The next morning, Tashira was riding her bike when she heard a voice crying. She looked and saw smoke pouring out of an open window. "Someone needs help," she thought. She jumped off her bike and ran to the window. Smoke stung her eyes, and she wanted to turn away, but she glimpsed a little boy inside crying for his mother.

CONTINUED

"I'll take you to her," Tashira told him. She reached through the window and pulled him out.

"Keisha's still in the house," he cried. Tashira looked through the window but the smoke was so thick, she could not see anything inside.

"Wait here," she cried. "We need more help." Tashira ran down the street. A moment later she was back with Officer Hamlette. He disappeared into the smoke. Tashira waited and waited. He was gone an awfully long time. When he finally came out of the house, he had a little girl in his arms. Now fire engines were roaring down the street with their sirens screaming. The firemen dashed into the house carrying long hoses.

The children's mother came running. "Oh my babies," she cried.

Reverend Wilburn came running. "Tashira, you're a hero!" he shouted. Then Tashira's teacher came running, "She's a hero!" she shouted. "Tashira's a hero."

A big crowd gathered around. Tashira's own mother was there to give her a big hug, too. "You're a hero, Tashira!" they all shouted.

Tashira just shook her head and smiled. "I'm not a hero," she said. "It's just my turn to help, that's all."

But everyone said she was a hero, all the same.

1. **What is the story mostly about?**
   - ○ **A** A girl sees everyone helping others and tries to do the same.
   - ○ **B** A police officer helps children in the playground.
   - ○ **C** A teacher helps paint the church.
   - ○ **D** A girl saves a young boy from a burning house.

2. **Which event in the story happens first?**
   - ○ **A** Tashira saves Keisha's brother.
   - ○ **B** Officer Hamlette gets a gang of boys to leave the playground.
   - ○ **C** Mrs. Jenkins helps Reverend Wilburn paint the steeple.
   - ○ **D** Tashira's mother scrubs a schoolyard wall.

3. **Which shows that Tashira's mother is helping out?**
   - ○ **A** She takes Tashira to school each morning.
   - ○ **B** She cleans a wall full of graffiti in the school yard.
   - ○ **C** She does spring cleaning at home.
   - ○ **D** She brings food to Officer Hamlette.

4. **The third paragraph states the "ugly words and pictures ran to the ground, where they turned into puddles of silver and gold." What does the author mean by "*puddles of silver and gold*"?**
   - ○ **A** The words and pictures were written with silver and gold ink.
   - ○ **B** The water in the puddle shimmered like silver and gold.
   - ○ **C** The puddles were extremely valuable.
   - ○ **D** The puddles had precious metals of gold and silver.

5. **What is the usual job of Mrs. Jenkins?**
   - ○ **A** Painter
   - ○ **B** Teacher
   - ○ **C** Police officer
   - ○ **D** Firefighter

6. **Why does Mrs. Jenkins decide to help Reverend Wilburn?**
   - A She owes him a favor.
   - B It is her turn to help out.
   - C Reverend Wilburn is afraid to climb so high.
   - D She needs to earn extra money on the weekends.

7. **"We're helping Reverend Wilburn." her teacher *proclaimed*. What does *proclaimed* mean?**
   - A Announce publicly
   - B Refuse to help
   - C Favor one side
   - D Show ownership

8. **Which best describes the people of Tashira's community?**
   - A They are very wealthy.
   - B They try to avoid hard work.
   - C They have a policeman because of frequent crimes.
   - D They assist other people who need help.

9. **"The *steeple* needs a fresh coat of paint." What is a *steeple*?**
   - A Basement of a building
   - B Tower on a church
   - C Main wall of a church
   - D Inside of a church building

10. **Why does Reverend Wilburn take dinner to Officer Hamlette and his family?**
    - A The church provides food for those too poor to buy their own.
    - B Officer Hamlette and his family have not eaten for days.
    - C Mrs. Hamlette just had a newborn baby.
    - D Mrs. Hamlette was badly hurt in a fire.

11. **Why did Tashira reach through the window of the smoking house?**
    - A She heard a girl in the house call for help.
    - B She saw a little boy in the house crying.
    - C She was visiting the people in the house.
    - D She wanted to show everyone she was a real hero.

12. **Why did Officer Hamlette enter the burning house?**
    - A He thought he could stop the fire.
    - B Tashira demanded that he enter the house.
    - C He tried to save the family's valuables.
    - D Tashira told him there was a child inside.

13. **Officer Hamlette and Tashira are similar in that they both**
    - A Play in the park
    - B Are brave and helpful
    - C Like to eat turkey
    - D Helped paint the church

14. **If Mrs. Jenkins became trapped on the church roof, what would you expect Officer Hamlette to do?**
    - A Send Tashira to call for extra help
    - B Call the fire department
    - C Climb up to rescue her
    - D Ask Reverend Wilburn to help her

15. **Why did people in the story call Tashira a hero?**
    - A She saved two children's lives.
    - B She ran into a burning house.
    - C She pushed past Officer Hamlette to save the baby.
    - D She helped save most of the main characters in the story.

16. Which statement is an opinion?
- A Some people in Tashira's community help others.
- B Tashira rides a bicycle.
- C Tashira was a hero.
- D The bad boys ran away from Officer Hamlette.

17. Why did Tashira tell everyone she was NOT a hero?
- A In her community, people helped out when it was their turn.
- B She ran for help instead of rushing into the house.
- C She did not really know what to do during the fire.
- D She had been afraid to save Keisha.

18. Which word best fits in Box 1?

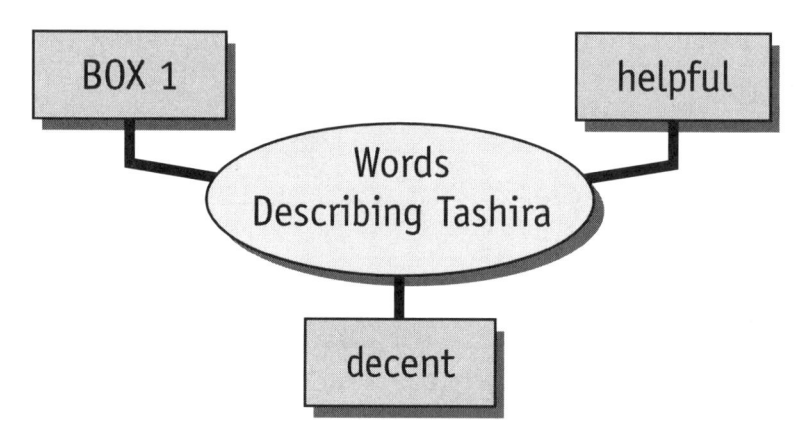

BOX 1 — helpful — decent → Words Describing Tashira

- A Cowardly
- B Greedy
- C Brave
- D Sad

19. What is the main theme of this story?
- A Children should not play with matches.
- B We should help others.
- C Always be careful around a fire.
- D Never judge people by the way they dress.

EXTENDED-RESPONSE QUESTION

20. How does Tashira show that she is brave in the story? Use information from the story and your own ideas to support your answer.

END OF SESSION 3

Chapter 19

A PRACTICE WRITING TEST

Directions: This writing test has three prompts. You will answer only *one* of these. Your teacher will tell you which prompt to answer.

WRITING PROMPT 1

Life is often filled with various celebrations. Sometimes we celebrate an event, like a birthday or a family wedding. At other times, we celebrate a national holiday like Thanksgiving.

Write a narrative paper that tells about a celebration you had with your family. Tell what you were celebrating, how you celebrated, and how you felt about it.

— OR —

WRITING PROMPT 2

Water is a very precious resource. We depend on water for many things. It is important to protect our sources of water.

Write an expository paper about how water is important to all of us. Explain how we use water and why it is important that we all do our part to protect our sources of water.

— OR —

WRITING PROMPT 3

Some parents allow their third-grade children to watch television during the week. Other parents allow their third-grade children to watch television only on weekends. Should third-graders be allowed to watch television on school days? Why or why not?

Write a persuasive paper telling whether you think children in third grade should be able to watch television on school days. Give reasons why you feel as you do.

APPENDIX

A HANDBOOK OF WRITING CONVENTIONS

The material in this Appendix provides a reference you can use to study for the test. The *Handbook of Writing Conventions* summarizes some of the basic rules third grade students are expected to apply in their writing.

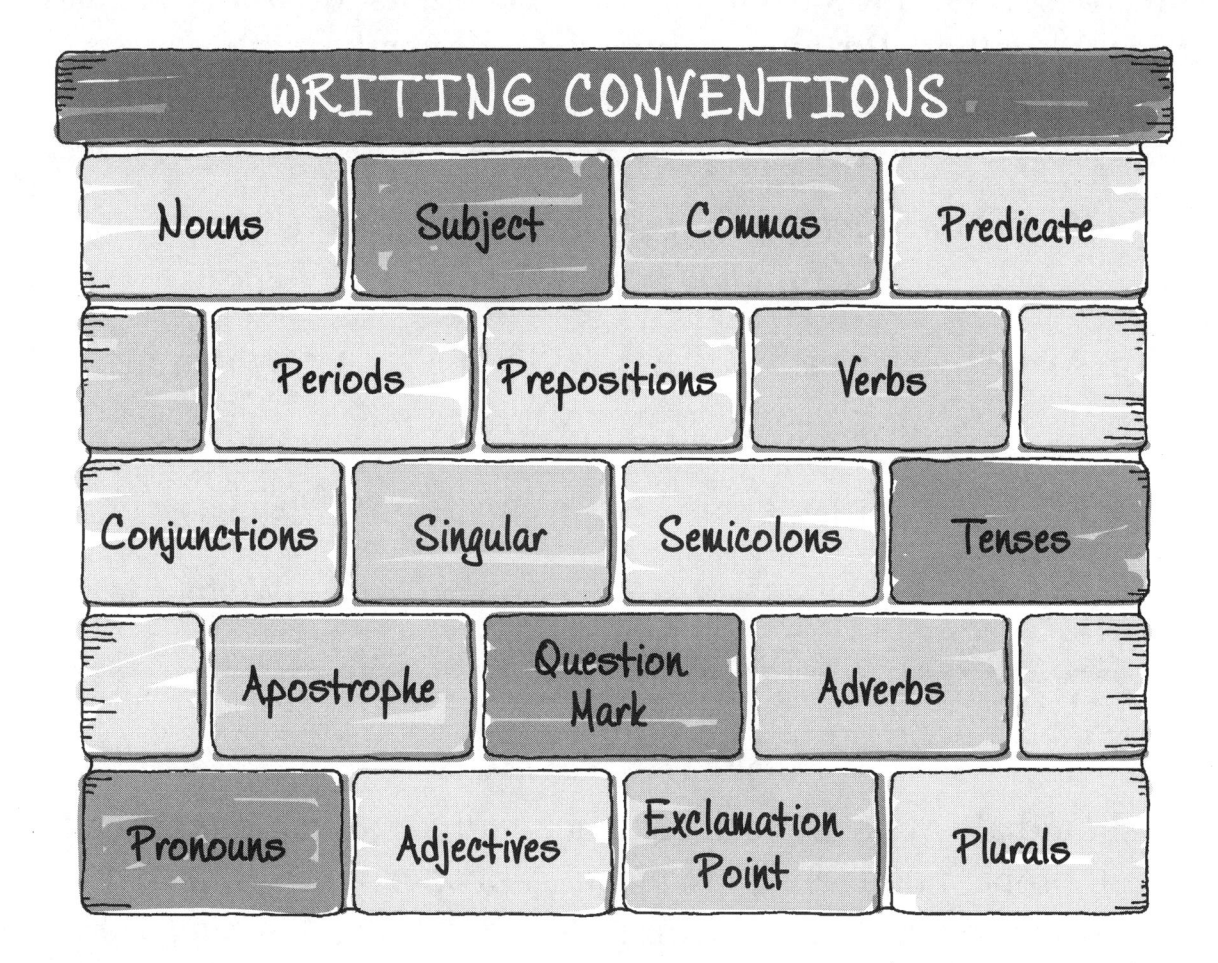

WRITING CONVENTIONS

- Nouns
- Subject
- Commas
- Predicate
- Periods
- Prepositions
- Verbs
- Conjunctions
- Singular
- Semicolons
- Tenses
- Apostrophe
- Question Mark
- Adverbs
- Pronouns
- Adjectives
- Exclamation Point
- Plurals

This handbook reviews some of the areas in which third graders sometimes make errors in writing conventions.

SPELLING

Hundreds of years ago there were no rules for spelling in English. People spelled each word in their own way. Today, we have rules for spelling words. Most words can be spelled in only one way.

Because the English language has been influenced by other languages, the same *sound* is not always spelled the same way. This makes it harder to know how to spell some words. When you misspell a word or learn a new word, you should look carefully at the word. Often there is a "hot spot" that makes the word difficult to spell. Focus on the "hot spot." Make a circle or box around it. Then write the word correctly several times from memory. Keep a list of words you have difficulty spelling. Practice spelling them correctly.

CHECKING YOUR UNDERSTANDING

Circle the "hot spot" in each of the following words. The first has been done for you.

T(ues)day	weather	balloon	swimming
across	coming	pleasant	address
their	friend	afraid	separate
receive	there	February	Wednesday

CAPITALIZATION

You should always start each sentence with a capital letter. In addition, all proper nouns are capitalized. A **proper noun** is the name of a specific person, place, or thing. For example, *Michael Jordan, Wheaton,* and the *Declaration of Independence* are all proper nouns.

APPENDIX: A HANDBOOK OF WRITING CONVENTIONS

CHECKING YOUR UNDERSTANDING

Underline each letter of the following nouns that should be capitalized.

- ★ mr. smith
- ★ florida
- ★ bread
- ★ meat loaf
- ★ strawberry jam
- ★ disneyland

PUNCTUATION

Here are some of the main rules for the correct use of punctuation:

★ Use commas to separate items in a list, dates, quotations, and places in a sentence where you would pause. Also use commas to separate a city from its state or country.

> Lenny brought tomatoes, eggs, milk, and a loaf of bread, to his hotel room in Paris, France.

★ Use periods at the end of abbreviations.

> Mr., Ms., Mrs., U.S.A.

★ Use apostrophes to show possession or contractions.

> Jack's boat   I'm = I am

★ Use quotation marks for direct speech.

> "I want to go home," she said loudly.

SENTENCE ENDINGS

You should always end a sentence with a *period, question mark,* or *exclamation point*. The punctuation you use will depend on the type of sentence you have written.

★ End each statement with a period.

> The hungry monkeys ate a bunch of bananas**.**

★ End each question with a question mark.

> What time is it**?**

★ End sentences that show strong feelings, such as surprise, laughter or some other strong emotion, with an exclamation point.

> You look absolutely ridiculous with that hat on your head**!**

CHECKING YOUR UNDERSTANDING

Add the final punctuation to each of these sentences.

★ The baker took the hot loaves of bread from the oven ☐

★ Where is the best place to buy a computer ☐

★ I have never been happier in all my life ☐

Insert the correct punctuation in the following paragraph:

It was late at night on October 13 ☐ 1995 ☐ Everything was quiet in the house ☐ Suddenly we heard a crash ☐ A large number of people rushed out of their homes to see what was going on ☐ ☐ Is anyone hurt ☐ ☐ our neighbor asked ☐ ☐ It looks like there was an earthquake ☐ ☐ my mother answered ☐

SUBJECT-VERB AGREEMENT

The subject and verb of a sentence should always "agree" with each other.

★ If the subject of a sentence is singular, you should use a verb in the singular form.

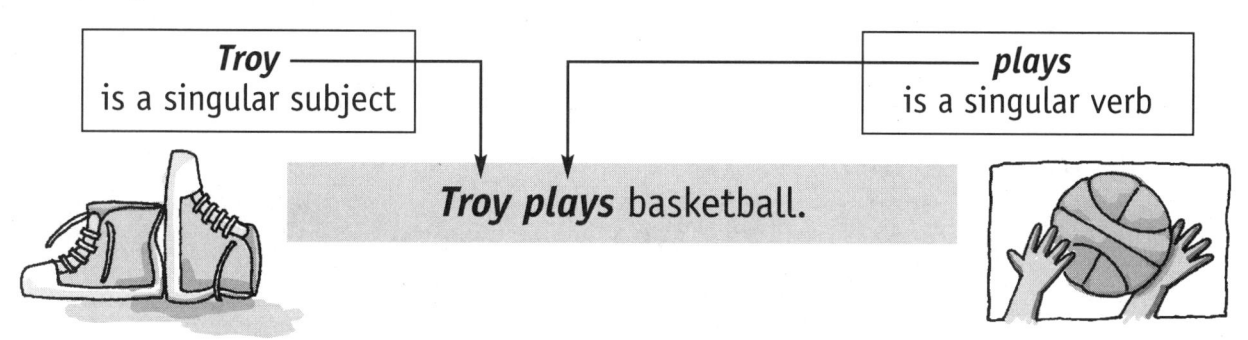

Troy is a singular subject

plays is a singular verb

Troy plays basketball.

★ If the subject of a sentence is plural, you should use a verb in the plural form.

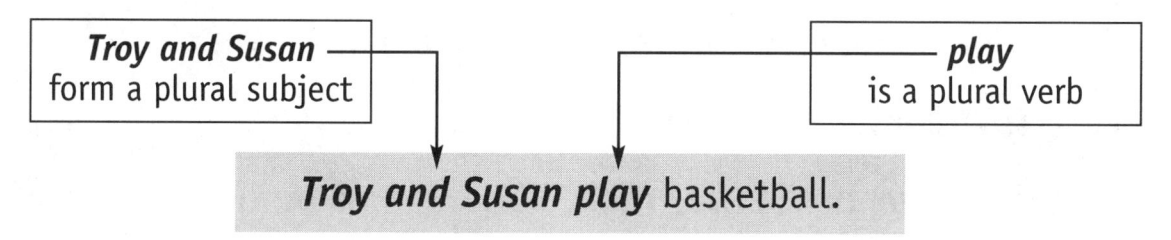

Troy and Susan form a plural subject

play is a plural verb

Troy and Susan play basketball.

CHECKING YOUR UNDERSTANDING

See if you can choose the correct verb in each of the following:

1. They (**are eating** / **is eating**) lunch.

2. They (**have** / **has**) many pets in their home.

3. He (**wakes** / **wake**) up each morning at 7:00 o'clock.

4. Susan's grandmother (**live** / **lives**) in Chicago, Illinois.

5. Joan (**walk** / **walks**) to school each morning.

PRONOUN FORMS

Pronouns take the place of nouns. Pronouns take different forms when they are used in different places in a sentence.

★ If the pronoun is the subject, use *I*, *you*, *he*, *she*, *it*, *we*, or *they*.

> **He** is going to karate class.

★ If the pronoun is not the subject of the sentence, use *me*, *you*, *him*, *her*, *it*, *us*, and *them*.

> Chinami gave **them** the present.
> Carson sent a birthday card to **her**.

CHECKING YOUR UNDERSTANDING

Select the correct pronoun to complete the following sentences:

1. (**He** / **Him**) went to the zoo for a visit.
2. (**She** / **Her**) baked (**he** / **him**) a cake for his birthday.
3. (**They** / **Them**) like to go bowling on Saturday.

Some pronouns raise special problems. Here are three groups that often cause confusion:

★ **It's / Its**

It's is a contraction for two words — *it* and *is*:

> **It's** time to go to bed.

Its without an apostrophe shows possession:

> The stray cat was missing **its** owner.

★ There / their / they're

There means a place: He lives over **there**.

Their shows possession: **Their** car is waiting.

They're is a contraction for two words — *they are*:

They're going away.

★ Your / You're

Your shows possession: Is this **your** boat?

You're means *you are*:   **You're** in a good mood today.

CHECKING YOUR UNDERSTANDING

Select the correct form of the word to complete the following sentences:

1. (***Its / It's***) time that we go home.
2. Is this (***your / you're***) hat and gloves?
3. (***There / Their / They're***) is where the monster lives.

VERB TENSES

Verbs take different forms, known as **tenses,** to tell us when an action takes place. Different tenses are used to express actions in the *present, past,* and *future*.

Past Tense	Present Tense	Future Tense
He liked her.	He likes her.	He will like her.
She was eating.	She is eating.	She will be eating.

When you write, be sure to keep your verbs in the right tense. If a story takes place in the past, keep all of the verbs you are using in the past tense. Change the tense of the verb only if the action moves to the present or future.

> Last week, the grumpy sailor *ate* at the old inn. He *had* a meal of fish and *washed* it down with some wine. Then he *went* to sleep in the loft in the stables above the horses. Next week, he *will go* back to work with the new captain of the ship.

Notice how the first three sentences are all happening in the past. In the last sentence, the action switches to something that will take place in the future. As a result, the verb changes to the future tense.